THE
APPROACH
TO
PREACHING

The

Approach

to

Preaching

BY

W. E. SANGSTER

M.A., Ph.D.

Minister of the Central Hall, Westminster

LONDON: THE EPWORTH PRESS

PUBLISHED BY

THE EPWORTH PRESS
(FRANK H. CUMBERS)
25–35 CITY ROAD, LONDON, E.C.1

*

New York . *Toronto*
Melbourne . *Capetown*

*

SET IN MONOTYPE BEMBO AND PRINTED IN
GREAT BRITAIN BY THE CAMELOT PRESS LTD.,
LONDON AND SOUTHAMPTON

TO

THE STAFF AND STUDENTS

AT

RICHMOND

DIDSBURY

HEADINGLEY

HANDSWORTH

HARTLEY–VICTORIA

AND

WESLEY HOUSE, CAMBRIDGE

in
Gratitude
for
a warm welcome
and
a patient hearing

What it means to be a priest can only properly be understood in Heaven. . . . If we sought to understand it on earth, we would have to die—not of fear but of love.

THE CURÉ D'ARS

My dear Son,

I would rather you were a preacher than Lord Chancellor of England.

DR. JOHN HUGHES TO HIS SON,
HUGH PRICE HUGHES

PREFACE

IN the year 1950 I was called to the Presidency of the Methodist Conference of Great Britain, and for a year, therefore, to the leadership of the Methodist Church in the British Isles. I conceived it to be part of my duty to visit the six Methodist theological colleges in England and talk to the future preachers of their work.

This book contains the substance of what I said, though the first lecture has been adapted (in writing) to a more general audience.

I am not without hope that the book will prove useful to other men preparing for the ministerial vocation, to those already in the work, and to the great army of lay preachers as well.

The warm welcome I received from Staff and Students at each of the Colleges, I acknowledge with gratitude in the Dedication, and it only remains for me to thank from my heart two who have helped me in different ways more than my halting words can ever express: the Rev. Dr. Charles Ryder Smith, and my unfailing Secretary, Mr. P. E. Found.

W. E. SANGSTER

The Central Hall
 Westminster
  London, S.W.1.

CONTENTS AND SUMMARY

The question is raised whether or not God calls men to be preachers, or whether it is all a pious pretence. Some men interested in the recruitment of the ministry think that most of the talk of a 'divine call' is confusing to candidates and had better be dropped. They urge that men be sought for the service of the Church as they are sought in other professions by a sensible set of vocational tests, and an extra stress on character.

Yet the Bible teaches that men are called of God to this work, and men in every generation have heard the call. They hear it still.

The difficulties of those who doubt a special call from God would be cleared up if it is recognized that God calls in different ways. 1. Sometimes the call is plainly heard. 2. Sometimes it is overheard. 3. Sometimes it comes through a felt need. Each of these ways is explained and illustrated. Counsel is given on how a man, still uncertain, might scrutinize himself and reach a conclusion.

Some elements in preaching defy analysis. Beyond homiletical technique there is something else: something vastly important. It can be called 'the plus of the Spirit' or 'unction'.

How can one get 'unction'? Being a gift of God, is the reception of it past understanding, or can we learn how to put ourselves in the way of receiving?

There is a three-fold preparation for this plus of the Spirit. 1. The Preparation of the Whole Life. 2. The Preparation of the Day. 3. The Preparation of the

Moment. The first is far the most important, and unction is shown to belong to devout men of all Communions. A clue is found in the longing for personal holiness, and a passion for lost souls.

Ministers are largely masters of their own time. It is both a privilege and a peril. They must develop a keen sense of time, learn to distinguish between ten minutes and a quarter-of-an-hour, employ the minutes spent in travel, avoid excessive social distractions, develop skill in dealing with time-wasters, and master business method.

To have still more time for the most important things one must: 1. Eliminate; 2. Delegate; 3. Cultivate. The things which belong under each heading are set out, and advice is given on how to achieve these desirable ends.

Gone are the days when people thought that only the sermon mattered in Divine Service. Every part of worship has an importance impossible to exaggerate. A plea is made for the 'free' form of service, and counsel offered on its every part. Nothing is small which helps or hinders people in their access to God: the minister's dress in the pulpit, his deportment, his own worshipful manner, the *order* and *wholeness* of the service.

Each in turn, the place and part of hymn-singing, prayer, Bible Reading, and silence is set out. How to lift the offertory into worship is shown, how to minimize the notices, and why we should abolish vespers.

The offices of preacher and pastor cannot be divorced. They belong together, and aid each other. The wide range of pastoral work is indicated and the way in which it feeds the pulpit is made plain.

What is the best place for the exercise of the pastor's

office? In the people's homes? In the minister's home? Or in the church vestry? Each has its special usefulness. All should be employed, but special stress is placed upon the use of the vestry for private interviews with people concerned about their soul.

The chief needs people bring to their minister are put in order. 1. Desire for a deeper Spiritual Experience. 2. Perplexities about their Prayer Life. 3. Intellectual Difficulties. 4. Domestic Incompatibility. 5. Nervous Disorders. 6. Loss of Zest for Church. 7. Sex Problems. 8. Desire to Confess their Sins.

Some ministers feel that they are failures in pastoral work, and hints are offered on how they might come to greater effectiveness.

Certain ailments are classified as 'occupational diseases'. The ministry has its occupational diseases as well. 1. Some temptations are not peculiar to the ministry, though they may come with special force because of the preacher's circumstances: women, money, laziness. 2. Some temptations (though not unknown outside the ministry) are nearer to being occupational diseases: the itch for popularity, jealousy, professionalism, intellectual snobbery, self-pity, pettiness, repenting our sacrifices, failing our children, neglecting our devotions. 3. Our occupational diseases, in the strictest sense of the words, however, are these: discharging a concern by preaching a sermon on it, and thinking ourselves Christlike because our people think it of us. How to avoid these perils is made plain throughout.

ONE

THE IMPERATIVE CALL

DOES God call men to be preachers of His good news, or is all this talk about 'a call' pious pretence?

Some men, who are interested in the recruitment of the ministry, think that it is pious pretence. At least, they are certain that a great deal of talk about 'a call' is exaggerated, that it bewilders humble men, takes no account of temperamental differences in candidates, and has excluded some most able people from the full-time service of God. The rare man who has had a dramatic call, they say, both simplifies and intensifies his experience in relating it, and erroneously implies that all men who are really called are called in a similar way. Some other men are tempted, therefore, to 'cook up' their own milder experiences on the assumption that this is what the Church expects, but how little they are called may be judged from the readiness with which some of them abandon the preacher's office when the testings and disappointments of the middle years come, or an alternative occupation presents itself, or the chance appears to secure a ministerial situation in which preaching is not the chief demand.

Having written novels while he was a minister of God, and gathered a 'public' large enough to convince him that he could live by novel-writing and lecturing alone, Silas K. Hocking left the ministry. He did it almost without a pang. He wondered afterwards if he had ever had a call, and wondered it also about some of his friends who were 'most certain of their divine call' at the time of candidature. Being called, Hocking concluded, is just doing 'the work that lies nearest at hand'.

Nor can it be doubted, say the people who would like all talk about 'a call' abandoned, that the word has been used by less scrupulous men to enter a profession which they judged to be easier to practise, or more socially distinctive, or more egotistically satisfying, than the one in which they found themselves before. They repeat the story of Booker T. Washington about the negro in Alabama who stopped work one hot day in the cotton-field, looked up at the sky, and said: 'O Lawd, de cotton am so grassy, de work am so hard, and de sun so hot, dat I believe dis darky am called to be a preacher.'

Let us drop all this talk about a distinctive 'call', say the critics, again, if only because it is admitted that God calls to other vocations besides the ministry, and let us seek men for the service of the Church in the same way that they are sought for in other professions. Is a man drawn to it? Does he have what it takes? Has he a sound character? Can he pass a sensible set of vocational tests? Very good! Train and ordain him. It is doubtful if we shall get inferior men this way, and we shall be saved from a great deal of the half-conscious pretending which goes under the word 'call'.

Admitting that there is something to be answered in these objections, it must be insisted, as we begin the reply, that the Bible emphatically teaches that God calls men to His ministry. Amos was called—and said so. So did Isaiah. Jeremiah's account of his call is moving in the extreme. Ezekiel is hardly less emphatic. Jesus called the Twelve. Perhaps the call of the apostle Paul is the most famous and classical of any. 'Necessity is laid upon me,' he said, and a thousand thousand men have known a similar inward compulsion in all the ages since.

Men hear the call today. It summons them from the Law Courts, and the office desk, and the schoolmaster's common room, the plough, and the mine, and the mill. At great personal sacrifice many of them answer the call. They say with Paul: 'Woe is unto me if I preach not the gospel.' Their friends often tell them of the quixotic folly of it, and urge them to make the service of God a spare-time occupation. It is all to no avail. 'I shall have no peace,' they say, 'unless I do this.' When all the weight of worldly wisdom has been marshalled against them, they make no effort at detailed answer and simply say: 'I am called.' The overwhelming number of those who say this answer the call and go on with their vocation—through constant testing and not infrequent disappointment—to the end of the road.

It would border on the ludicrous in the face of all this evidence to deny the call of God in the soul of man simply because a few men have pretended to a call they never received, or disregarded a genuine summons when they found the way hard, or saw a by-path later more suited to their love of lucre and of comfort.

Nor must it be forgotten that the recollection of his call is one of the chief means by which a man is kept faithful to a task which is, by common consent of all who are informed, one of the very hardest in the modern world. A business man given a sudden insight into the character of an able minister's full life, and knowing him to be overworked and underpaid, must often have wondered why the man went on with his work at such slight material reward and with other openings at hand which he could easily enter. 'He can't be doing it for what he gets. If he wanted the pleasure of hearing himself speaking, he must be tired of that long ago. If he took up the work at first to please his parents, that can't be holding him at present. And it is a hard, frugal life for his wife as well. I wonder why he does it?'

He was called, sir: he was called.

It must not, however, be supposed that God always calls in one way. There is point in the contention of the critics that the man called with dramatic suddenness is in danger of implying that God's call always comes that way. Certain it is that many earnest men drawn to offer themselves to God and His Church have hesitated to do so because they have expected to be laid hold of by God in ways He does not always use.

God calls, I think, in three chief ways.

I

The call of God comes to some people in an utterly unmistakable way. They are, in Paul's phrase, 'apprehended by Christ Jesus': arrested, almost, by Heaven: called by their name: selected and chosen. This is the call, I suppose, *par excellence*. This is the call which most men wish in their heart could be theirs.

It was like that with Paul. How many times we have meditated upon him hurtling along the road to Damascus, bent upon dragging all those who had committed themselves to Christ, to prison and to death.

Suddenly there was a light above the brightness of the sun: a light blinding in its intensity; and a voice which spoke to him in Hebrew and called him by his name: 'Saul, Saul, why persecutest thou me?' And in answer to his bewildered question as to who it was who called, the answer came: 'I am Jesus whom thou persecutest. . . .'

That is the call of God in its supremest and most unmistakable way. It is an overwhelming experience to fall thus into the hands of the living God: to be invaded to the depths of one's being by His presence: to be, without warning, wholly uprooted from one's old, secure vocation: to see, as with the eye of vision, on the one hand the world of struggling, sinful, earth-blinded men and nations, and, on the other, in awful solemnity, the Holy One, tenderly loving, infinitely patient, inexorable in His call. Under such an experience, one cries like the convinced Thomas of old, with all doubt burned out of one's soul: 'My Lord and my God.'

The call to preach came to Mrs. Booth, the mother of the Salvation Army, almost as suddenly as that. Her husband was a Methodist minister at the time in Gateshead. She was a shy, nervous, timid woman, who had never spoken in public: had hardly ever imagined herself speaking in public. Here is her own account of how the call to preach came to her. She says:

> *I was, as usual on a Sunday morning, in the minister's pew with my eldest boy, then four years old. I felt much depressed in mind and was not expecting anything particular . . . but I felt the Holy Spirit come upon me. It seemed as if a Voice said to me: 'Now, if you were to come and testify, you know I would bless it to your own soul as well as to the people.' I gasped and said in my heart, 'Yes, Lord, I believe Thou wouldst, but I cannot do it. . . .' I felt as though I would sooner die than speak. And then the devil said, 'Besides, you are not prepared. You would look a fool and have nothing to say.' He made a mistake. He over-reached himself for once. It was this word that settled it. 'Ah!' I said, 'This is just the point. I have never yet been willing to be a fool for Christ. Now I will be one.'*

B

Without staying another moment, I rose from my seat and walked down the aisle. My dear husband was just going to conclude. He thought something had happened to me, and so did the people. We had been there two years and they knew my timid, bashful nature. He stepped down and asked me: 'What is the matter, my dear?' I replied: 'I want to say a word.' He was so taken by surprise he could only say: 'My dear wife wants to speak', and sat down. For years he had been trying to persuade me to do it. Only that very week he had wanted me to go and address a little cottage meeting of some twenty working people, but I had refused.

All the world knows what happened after that. Wonders attended her speaking from the very beginning: in Gateshead, in Hartlepool, and everywhere else. The denominational journal made constant references to the astonishing effects of her preaching, and those who were prejudiced against women speaking, came and were convinced.

It was the call of God: direct, unmistakable, addressed to her by name. That is the call, I suppose, all people in their heart secretly long for. But let me say quite definitely, that it isn't the call which all men receive.

II

If anyone were to ask why God doesn't always call in that peremptory way, I would not know the answer. I only know He doesn't. I only know that those of us who are parents, dealing with our own children, know that there are temperamental differences in them. One child can be summoned by the quietest word simply spoken, and another, it seems, must receive a peremptory command. Only God Himself knows why the call must be in one tone with one person, and in another tone with the next.

But *it is still the call of God*, even if it is not so seemingly supernatural and arresting.

Think of the call of Isaiah. God never addressed Isaiah by name. Indeed, it would almost seem as though Isaiah overheard a remark which God made to the angels or uttered in soliloquy. When, in vision, he saw the temple and the Lord sitting upon the throne, he was so awed by the presence of the Almighty and by the seraphim and, most of all, by his own uncleanness, that if any word had been spoken to him directly it would have been more, I imagine, than he could endure.

But he says: 'And I heard the voice of the Lord saying' —not to him, but to the seraphim one must suppose, or to Himself—'Whom shall I send, and who will go for us?' And Isaiah broke in, murmuring: 'Here am I; send me.' And God said: 'Go.'

The call of God still comes in that indirect way. It is still possible to overhear God speaking to someone else. Men have heard the missionary advocates telling about the immense need of the overseas field. It may never have crossed their mind that the word was spoken to them. Perhaps it wasn't. They may have thought, and you may have thought, that the word was being directed to somebody else; somebody with five talents burnished bright; somebody with natural gifts or early advantages which you have never had. It was not said to you, but you overheard it.

What are you going to do about it? Dare you go to the Almighty and say, as Isaiah did, 'Here am I; send me'? Is it possible that the Almighty might say to you, as He said to Isaiah, 'Go'?

Or the call may pull a man from the overseas field to the work at home.

When Dr. Barnardo left Dublin for London, he went of set purpose to train as a missionary for China. That was his whole aim in going to London. Later, he decided to be a medical missionary and entered the London Hospital. As an occupation of his scanty leisure, he started a meeting for poor boys, and that was how he met Jim Jarvis. The main service at the little mission was over one evening and one laddie lingered behind. It was Jim Jarvis.

'Go home, Jim', said the medical student. And still Jim lingered.

'It's getting late; go home, Jim', said Barnardo. And still Jim stayed behind. Half losing his patience, Barnardo said, 'Won't you go home, Jim?'

And Jim said: 'Please, sir, I haven't a home to go to.' It was true.

Barnardo heard God remark that evening, concerning the homeless boys of London and His pitying heart towards them: 'Whom shall I send, and who will go for us?' But Barnardo took no notice because, of course, he was going to China.

Sometime later, he met Lord Shaftesbury at a dinner and he told Lord Shaftesbury about the need of the East End, and Lord Shaftesbury—not unnaturally—was unwilling to believe the statements that Barnardo made without proof. To put the matter to a test, the whole party rose up from the dinner table, and got into hansom cabs and drove to Whitechapel to see if Barnardo could prove his point. So he led them to a goods' shed where the various items of merchandise were covered by tarpaulins, where everything was absolutely quiet and desolate, and where nobody but Barnardo himself was expecting the revelation which ensued. The young medical student pushed his hands between two packing-cases, got hold of the naked feet of a little boy and pulled him out. When the little lad was told that they were not the police but only wanted to know if the East End was alive with homeless boys, he consented to find plenty more in the same condition, and he started to jump on the tops of the packing cases all around him. In a few moments seventy-three homeless boys were discovered in that one spot alone. The year was 1866 in Christian England.

Barnardo overheard God speaking again: 'Whom shall I send, and who will go for us?' Lord Shaftesbury heard it too. He turned to Barnardo and said: 'Are you sure that it is China He is sending you to?'

Barnardo listened again: 'Whom shall I send, and who will go for us?'

And—not without pain and sacrifice—Barnardo made mighty answer: 'Here am I; send me,' and God said: 'Go.'

That was not a call to the ordained ministry but God calls preachers in the same indirect way.

Can you overhear the call of God at this time? He may appear to be addressing the question to someone else. It may, indeed, be His indirect approach. Listen! May it not be meant for you, though it is not *said* to you? Are you ready to say: 'Here am I; send me'?

III

Even that does not exhaust all the ways in which God calls us. Sometimes He does not speak directly to us as He did to Paul, and sometimes He doesn't speak indirectly as He did to Isaiah. Sometimes He just shows us the need. Nothing else. Just makes us to see the necessity for it and says, in effect, through the need: 'You know Me; you know My purposes in the world; you know that this is an affront and a pain to Me: do you need to know any more?'

When I was a lad at home, I sometimes defended myself for neglecting the little duties of the home by saying: 'Well, nobody *told* me to do it.' My father, I remember, always seemed more than a little annoyed at my defence. Before Mother could reply, he would break in and say: 'Did you *need* to be told? You could see that it needed doing. It was plain before your eyes. Must you always be *told*?'

I sometimes think God deals with us like that. I sometimes wonder if, when we get to heaven, and realize the pain of God that in the presence of such great need in this world we did nothing about it, or hardly anything, and seek to make some feeble defence about 'not being clearly called', I sometimes think He will look on us and say: 'Did you need to be called? Was not the need itself loud enough in your ears?'

God does not always arrest us in the way that He did Paul. There is, at times, a wonderful reticence in God. He treats us on occasion as the Stranger on the road to Emmaus treated those two men with whom He walked in company. And even when He is at the door, He makes as though He would go farther and only lingers when we plead with Him to come in.

Has it been like that with you? Has He treated you with a similar reticence? Has He shown you the need and left it to your own sense of spiritual values? Isn't it enough? Can you not find a call just in that?

The name of Wendell Phillips may be known to you. He was one of the greatest orators America ever produced. He trained himself to be an orator in order to practise law. He had no other purpose in so doing. But one October day he saw an American citizen brutally assaulted because he had dared to champion the cause of the slave, and Wendell Phillips saw the task to which, though he heard no voice from heaven to himself or to another, he dared believe that God had called him, and he dedicated all his days and all his powers to the abolition of slavery and to justice for the coloured man.

God never called Florence Nightingale in the way that He called Paul. She never overheard Him talking to the angels as Isaiah did. She just saw the need: sick and wounded men in an age when the typical nurse, as Charles Dickens made clear, was a Mrs. Gamp; indolent, drunken, and not seldom a prostitute. God permitted Florence Nightingale to see the need, and that vision was call enough for her consecrated soul.[1]

These illustrations are not of preachers, but again the call can come to preachers simply out of a recognized need.

'What is the most urgent need in the world today?' a young man might ask himself, and it would not be surprising, in a world like this, if he concluded that nothing is so needed, and nothing so urgent, as the triumph of moral and spiritual values. If, moreover, that young man were convinced that there was no hope of these values triumphing except by the power of Jesus Christ, would it be strange if he decided to give the one life he has to give to the proclamation of this gospel?

It will be objected to this reasoning that this is *not* a Divine call. The man is choosing himself. He will lack in any hour of depression, the very comfort I have

[1] There were, however, four occasions in her life when Florence Nightingale claimed to hear God's voice. (Cecil Woodham Smith, *Florence Nightingale*, p. 17.)

already described as necessary, i.e. the unshaken assurance that he was called.

But there is an answer even to that.

The work of the ministry is preceded, in most Communions, by the opportunity of Christian service for a layman. As Local Preacher, or Lay Reader, or Youth Leader, the Church provides opportunity for the man not yet ordained to test his call. Here are the questions a man who has received no imperative call might put to his soul in order to test whether or not the need alone is summoning him and the Divine approval rests upon his offering.

Does my desire to give myself entirely to this work grow ever stronger and stronger in me? Is it a *stable* desire—not changing as do the whims of boys, who fancy themselves in one calling this week and in another the next, but a constant sense of vocation set like a compass needle always towards the magnetic north?

Do I believe whole-heartedly in the Gospel?

Have I gifts for the work? This does not mean, of course, 'am I free of all nervousness at the prospect of it?' The more humble a man is, the more nervous he might well be. Indeed, it is probable that he will always remain nervous to some extent. There is value in that nervousness. It helps to keep a man on the knees of his soul. It 'tunes' him up for his work like the tautening of the strings of the violin before the player begins. The question is strictly: 'Have I gifts for the work?' Do I love people and want to win them for Christ? Can I hold an audience? Have I a reasonable freedom in speech? Have I the will and ability to apply myself to study?

Has my 'prentice preaching had any fruits? Do I know of people changed to God through the word I have spoken, or has God used me to win them by personal evangelism when worship was over? Have wise Christian friends persistently urged me to offer?

Have the people of God been nourished by the bread of heaven as I have broken it? Have unsurrendered sinners been made more miserable, and sad souls comforted, and perplexed people guided by God's use of my word?

Have I the physical fitness the work demands? This does not mean, of course, 'Am I a Hercules?' It is amazing what use God has made in the ministry of men of whom doctors of medicine have entertained doubts. Even defects of speech are sometimes gloriously overcome. I know two most able preachers both of whom were bad stammerers in their boyhood. Only the slightest trace of it remains now, and the trace (in the judgement of some people) adds charm to their words.

But a man with an uncured cleft palate should put the ministry out of his mind. God has other work for him to do.

If a man can pass the test of these and similar questions in the white light of God, let him go forward boldly. After all, the last word is not his. The Church must confirm his call. Let him offer himself, and tell those appointed to examine him that he *believes* he is called. If they concur in his judgement, let him not hesitate because no Damascus vision blinded his eyes and because —unlike Isaiah—he did not overhear the Lord conferring with the seraphim. Let him venture onwards, trusting God to add inward confirmation to the call of his heart and of the Church, until he too can say with a certitude not less than those who came by other ways: 'I was called.'

TWO

THE PLUS OF THE SPIRIT

IT is admitted by all who have closely studied the high task of preaching that there are elements of mystery in it which defy analysis. When all has been said that can be said about sensitivity to God's guidance in the choice of a theme; about the structure of the sermon itself; about the power of illustration and simplicity in language; about making contact with the congregation and moving with swift, firm steps to one's climaxes . . . there is still a mystic element which eludes all explanation but in which the moving power of the sermon unquestionably rests.

This can be proven in two ways. There are men who are superb masters of the craft of preaching who cannot move people—except for the moment, and normally to admiration of the preacher himself. There are others who are not masters of the craft: who make crass homiletical blunders and are plainly ill-informed in some ways, but who bring an awe-ful sense of God with them and whose sermons may leave a man for ever different. Fortunately, this is not an 'either—or'. How to have both—the craft, and this indefinable plus of the Spirit— should be the aim of every man who comes with consecration to the service of the pulpit.

Nobody has ever been able to define this quality which I have called 'the plus of the Spirit', but it can be felt even though it cannot be defined. I do not suggest that those who lack this peculiar quality in preaching have no help from the Holy Spirit at all. That would be foolish and, indeed, blasphemous. From the moment when a text or theme first fastens on our heart, we have the aid of the Spirit and, so eager is He to save, that every utterance which can be called Christian preaching is attended by the Blessed Paraclete. But there are times when He is present in especial power. It does not depend entirely upon the preacher. Congregations have their own important part to play in this—but it is as preachers that we are approaching the matter now and it would be spiritually profitable if we supposed that under God it all depends on us. Lightly to explain the absence of that mystic something which Paul called 'with demonstration of the Spirit and with power' as due to a deficiency in the congregation, would be vain in any preacher. 'What can *I* do', the humble minister of God might well ask himself, 'to be sure that the Holy Spirit has free course on every occasion when I rise to preach?' Or do the facts compel us to conclude that the matter is wrapped in too much mystery ever to be pierced and we can only say, 'The Spirit bloweth where it listeth'?

The nearest word to define what we are seeking is the word 'unction'. The word has been defaced by current misuse and is commonly confused today with 'unctuousness'. But, in its earlier and stricter use, it came nearest to defining this 'plus of the Spirit', and it has no synonym.

In the absence of a serviceable word to define what we mean, we can only describe and illustrate it. It is not to be confused with oratorical gifts. Men have oratorical gifts which can powerfully impress a congregation, but no unction. Men have unction with no oratorical gifts.

It is not to be confused with what people call 'personality' in a preacher. In the first place, nobody seems able to define what he means by that over-used word 'personality', but when he illustrates it by saying: 'That man . . . and that man . . . has personality', it is clear that he is not illustrating 'the plus of the Spirit'. Men in the pulpit sometimes have a striking uniqueness of nature which impresses their hearers but it is not unction. Men have unction who are not 'personalities' at all.

Men with unction impress others as having the breath of God about them. The spiritually sensitive know it at once: even the spiritually insensitive are often aware of a strange difference which they cannot explain. People of discernment are conscious that there is a Divine element operating in the preaching: the preacher seems to fade out and leave the hearers face to face with God.

That this mystic element may be present (as I have said) in those unskilled in the structure of sermons and speeches, could be illustrated from a multitude of men but let a couple of instances suffice—one from the west side of the Atlantic and one from the east.

In his early days as a preacher, and long before he had any mastery of homiletics, Matthew Simpson displayed the unction which marked his preaching throughout life. He said himself of those days:

> *I did not try to make sermons. I felt I must, at the peril of my soul, persuade men to come to Christ: I must labour to the utmost of my ability to get sinners converted, and believers advanced in holiness. For this I thought and studied, wept and fasted and prayed. My selection of words, my plan of discourse, was only and all the time to persuade men to be reconciled to God. I never spoke without the deepest feeling, and unless I saw a strong, divine influence on the congregation, I felt sad, and sought retirement to humble myself before God in prayer.*

From the English side of the Atlantic, I select Thomas Cook, an evangelist whose chief work was done in the last quarter of the nineteenth century and who, despite evangelistic tours in four continents, was little known outside his own church. Not even his friends claimed that, like Simpson, he had outstanding gifts. Indeed, it is astonishing how many people who sought to explain the power he could exert over a congregation began by saying: 'He was such an *ordinary* person.'

Thomas Cook was going to preach at a certain church over one week-end, and the friends who were to entertain him were so happy at the prospect of his coming that, long before the day arrived, they sickened the maid by the constant mention of his name. Collecting the joint at the butcher's on the Saturday morning, the irreverent girl mentioned the unnecessary fuss and said to the butcher: 'You would think that Jesus Christ was coming.'

Thomas Cook came, and conquered the girl (as he had conquered thousands of others by the breath of God which seemed always to be about him), and when he appealed in the Sunday evening worship for an open avowal of discipleship from any who would make it, the maid came out.

Tuesday morning found her at the butcher's again, and the butcher, remembering her blasphemy three days before, asked the girl with a grin if Jesus Christ had come.

With awful earnestness she answered: '*Yes. He came.*'

Cook did that or, rather, the Spirit did it through him. I never heard him preach but I have questioned scores of people who did. He was not singular in possessing this power, though I think it is less common than once it was. But he is a satisfying illustration because, by common agreement, he had none of the gifts which people

suppose to be essential to powerful preaching. He had no
commanding presence, organ voice, or unusual homiletical skill. He gave all he had but his gifts of nature
were not large. It was 'the plus of the Spirit' which
explained his all but irresistible power in preaching, and
his example should incite the least-endowed of men to
seek this gift from God.

Few things militate more against the revival of preaching than the commonly accepted idea that to be an
effective preacher one must possess certain gifts of nature
not widely given. Too many men in their middle years,
who once told the fathers of the Church that they were
called by God to preach the gospel, have been trapped
by their disappointments into believing that it is all a
matter of special gifts and, because they do not possess a
fluency, or an imagination, or an eloquence given to
others, can never expect to be powerful in preaching.
All this is tantamount to shutting out the Holy Spirit. If
we are driven to make comparisons, we must insist that
grace-gifts are more important than natural gifts. It is
true that the gift of the Holy Spirit works on the gifts of
nature, but it is true also that the Holy Spirit can work
on very little and, if *effectiveness* is borne in mind rather
than popularity, the unction of the Spirit is the greatest
gift of all.

Granted this, ordinary men can do extraordinary
things. So equipped, even those who have, what Kant
called, 'a step-motherly nature', can be most effective for
God, while those at whose birth all the fairies were
present, have the supernatural extra without which their
fine endowments will do nothing that can endure.

Is it now possible for us to attempt an answer to the
question: 'How is this gift received?'

Clearly, it *is* a gift. No man earns or compels the

Spirit. It is given rather than gained. When we have allowed for the element of mystery which will always attend the reception of this blessing, surely it is possible to understand something about putting ourselves in the way of receiving it and how to avoid those errors which will effectively shut it out.

There is, I think, a three-fold preparation for this plus of the Spirit in preaching. Not each part of the preparation is equally important, nor does each call for equal treatment here. But the preparation is three-fold:

1. The Preparation of the Whole Life.
2. The Preparation of the Day.
3. The Preparation of the Moment.

Let us look at each of them in turn.

I. THE PREPARATION OF THE WHOLE LIFE

The secret we are seeking—so far as it can be humanly understood—is in this section of our subject. Something of the man himself goes over in preaching. It is not chiefly in what he says. It is not only in the over-tones of his way of saying it: it is more tenuous even than this. His mind and heart reach out and touch the hearts and minds of those who hear him and, beyond the power of preacher or hearers to analyse, there is a meeting. That is why some teachers of homiletics insist that preaching is not the making and delivery of sermons but the making and delivery of a *man*. Always in preaching there is a giving of the self. Those who are closest to God, the channels of whose life are clean enough to be the channels of the Holy Spirit, are, by the very orderings of heaven, chosen vessels to bear His name before the people with all the power of that unction which is only from above.

Unction cannot be faked. When the attempt is made, and unctuousness results, men resist it as completely as they are subdued by the real thing. Their contempt for the counterfeit is proportionate to their admiration for the Divine quality it is pretending to be. It is felt to be hypocrisy of the worst order.

Something of what a man is 'in the inward parts' comes over in preaching. Bearing in mind again the distinction between effectiveness and popularity (though the two are, of course, not necessarily disparate), it may be said, against all the superficial contradictions, that it is not great ability which ultimately subdues men but great goodness. Many illustrations could be given. The Curé D'Ars had no great ability. His professors gave so poor an account of his seminary career that they never expected the Bishop to call him. His brother priests in the diocese actually attempted to have him unfrocked for his palpable ignorance of theology. Yet, by this poor instrument, the Holy Spirit changed Ars. The picture of the Curé weeping in the pulpit over the wayward members of his flock and asking them how they thought he could ever enjoy heaven if they were in hell, lets light in on the mystery. Those who have unction have an aching love for souls. It is one of their marks. We shall see it in preachers both Romanist and Reformed, and it will serve as a mark of its entry into our own poor hearts.

The Bible makes no secret of the fact that Moses was no orator. His brother Aaron was the orator. Moses was 'slow of speech', but was chosen, nonetheless, as the vehicle of God's word. Pusey was no orator. Even his friends admit so much. He read his sermons in the pulpit —and not particularly well. But, hard as his theological opponents might find it to believe, he had unction.

The facts compel us to believe, therefore, that there is

a traceable connection between this 'plus of the Spirit' in preaching and a man's secret life of intimate communion with God. It is not found, for instance, in those preachers (however great their natural gifts and attractive powers) whose flights of oratory in public prayer are unmatched by any private wrestling with God. What we are in the secret recesses of our soul affects our reception of this extra endowment. It is concerned with private prayer; the strength, and the length, and the unselfishness of it. It is concerned with brooding on God's Book: not for texts to preach on but for pastures to feed in. It is concerned with faithful self-examination, conducted in the white light of God, and an utter mercilessness with all discovered sin. It is concerned with the authority of first-hand religion: personal, positive, glowing experience of God, which gives power to a man's utterance and sets the hall-mark of truth on all he says.

No one can have unction without this. No preacher who has this will really be without the Spirit's special power.

If it is said that unction is rare, and my analysis suggests a poverty in the devotional life of many preachers, I can only say, in oscillating shame and thanksgiving, that I know in experience that, when my own devotional life is scamped, authority goes out of the Word I am given to deliver, and when, in penitence, I pray myself close to God again, He adds a plus once more. There are *degrees* in which we receive this grace-gift. None of us, we may hope, is an entire stranger to it.

> *For more we ask; we open then*
> *Our hearts to embrace Thy will;*
> *Turn, and revive us, Lord, again,*
> *With all Thy fullness fill.*

C

Is it possible to focus still more sharply the character of the devotional life of those who conspicuously enjoyed this gift?

Two things have struck me in my scrutiny of the lives of those who had it—so far as scrutiny is ever possible of another man's private life with God. These favoured souls had received from God an unusual quality of personal holiness, and they had been given a passionate love of souls. These similarities overleap all barriers of denomination. Superficially, there is not much that is alike between Jean-Marie Vianney and Thomas Cook. In point of fact, to those who know their lives with intimacy, their master passions were precisely the same: for holiness and for lost souls.

Two small towns face each other across the Lake of Geneva: Nyon and Thonon. Both are connected with a saint. John de la Flechere was born at Nyon, and St. Francis de Sales not far from Thonon. A superficial acquaintance with their careers would suggest few similarities between them (even if a de la Flechere *was* chosen as godfather to the infant Francis!), but the eye of the reverent student pierces beneath the differences to the deep alikeness of these two holy men. John de la Flechere made his way to England to become John Fletcher ('the seraphic Fletcher'), John Wesley's colleague, and designated successor in the leadership of the Methodist people, student and exponent of perfection, whose memorial sermon Wesley preached from the text: 'Mark the perfect man.' And Francis grew up to be 'the man of the world' who was also a saint, to bear later the august title bestowed upon him by the Church, 'Doctor of Perfection'. Holiness and lost souls were the master motives of them both. Could they have met in life, each would have felt that the other was in grievous theological error, but when they met by the Throne it was with mutual understanding and the ardour of love.

Holiness and lost souls! Those who seek from God, in the privacy of their own heart and chamber, purity in the inward parts and an aching passion for the wayward souls of men, will find that, in giving them these, God gives them a glorious extra—this mystic 'plus of the Spirit', the secret of which we have been seeking here. Holiness in our inward life comes out in indefinable ways in our pulpit life. The melting care of souls comes out as well. The words may falter and stumble but something will burn its way into the brains of the wanderers: 'This is a man of God. He loves us. He loves us *dearly*....' They will not call it 'unction'. They do not use the word but, against the weight of their own sinning, they will begin to eye the road which leads to home.

2. THE PREPARATION OF THE DAY

Less important than the preparation of one's whole life, but not without its importance in the quest we are now on, is the preparation of the day itself. The Lord's day comes with swift regularity to the preacher, and can find the man who has left his preparation late in a fever of apprehension. On rare occasions, any man may be late with his sermon, and late for reasons good enough to be given to God. An epidemic may have increased his pastoral visitation to inordinate dimensions; or sickness in his own family circle may have broken his nights and invaded his days; or the business cares of the church may have been unusually demanding. If he can look God in the face with his reasons, he need not fear to face his congregation. Special help is given in special need.

But when a man has frittered time, and knows it:

when lack of method, and disregard of priorities,
accounts for his unready state to preach the word of God:
when he turns again to stuff prepared for other congregations years ago, or hastily flings down a few thoughts
which can be spread out thin for twenty minutes, that
man is undeserving of special help from God . . . and
he knows it too. He carries on his shoddy 'preparation'
to the very moment of leaving for church, and not the
least serious of his faults is that the preparation of his
message has excluded any serious preparation of himself.

Geniuses do not fit into normal patterns. Beecher
prepared both his sermons on the day of their delivery.
Spurgeon prepared his morning sermon on Saturday
evening, and his evening sermon on Sunday afternoon,
but 'preparation' as used here of both these pulpit giants
really amounted to nothing more than making the final
outline. The matter had been yeasting in their minds
most of the week, and the 'preparation' here described was
largely deciding what line to take with all this material,
and what to leave out.

Nor could it be justly said of either of them that they
did not prepare *themselves*. Indeed, their very methods
required a fuller preparation of themselves than the
methods of those who—though they do not read—have
a manuscript behind all they say.

Leave that aside. Those who are deeply concerned
about the 'plus of the Spirit' in preaching must be particular about the preparation of themselves. It is best
for normal men to have the sermon made and out of the
way *before* Sunday. A quiet conning of the notes should
be enough on the day itself so far as the message is concerned. The pre-service hour, or half hour, should be a
time of quiet with God; of prayer and directed meditation; of being further sensitized to the Spirit's guiding;

of getting that greater openness to heaven which makes one alert to any re-shaping of the message or new application of its truth. It is patently foolish to covet the Spirit's power in what we are to say unless, in quiet waiting, we seek assurance that we know what the message really is.

I suggest that we prepare ourselves on the day of action by a three-fold meditation.

1. *Let a man think, first, on Christ.* Let him ask himself Whose servant he is: Whose commission he holds: Whose message he has to deliver. Let him think on the eagerness of his Lord to bless, and how concerned He is to use the message and give His servant true success. Let him be awed, but not overwhelmed, by his responsibilities: aware of his own weakness, but aware of God's power.

2. *Let him think, secondly, on the people.* Let the pageant of their piteous need pass before his eyes: their heart-breaks, temptations, disappointments, and courage. Let him think on all that can happen to one mortal in one service. Between 11 a.m. and 12.15 p.m. God converted Spurgeon and called him to be a preacher. Between 7 p.m. and 8.30 p.m. God lifted Wilfred Grenfell from atheism to faith and set him on the road which led to Labrador. God's greatest miracle happens often under preaching. Let a man think on the eternal consequences of one half hour.

3. *Let him think, finally, and most briefly, on himself.* Let him be utterly sure that his own reputation as a preacher is not in his mind, and that on the fringe of his sub-conscious he is not inquiring: 'How well am I going to do? I wonder what they will think of me today?' Let his inner peace revolve around two foci: his personal unimportance, seeing that everything at the last depends

upon Another, and the importance of his openness to Heaven if the occasion is to be made a maximum for God.

In this three-fold meditation, varied according to circumstances, but all directed to opening one's soul to the Holy Spirit, lies, as it seems to me, the preparation of the day itself.

3. THE PREPARATION OF THE MOMENT

Jenny Lind was a devout woman. People of spiritual discernment knew it, and people without spiritual discernment often guessed it. She sought to sing always to the glory of God.

A few moments before her call came in any concert, she excluded everybody from her dressing-room and locked the door. She would stand quietly in the centre of the room and softly strike a note. As the note filled the room, she lifted her heart to Christ and offered her prayer: 'Let me sing true tonight.' Her own explanation of her astonishing world-wide success—that something extra which all people conceded that she had—was the conscious sense of her Master's presence whenever she sang.

No preacher can be alone the moment before he gives out his text. Normally, he has been leading the worship of the people for forty minutes before this solemn moment comes.

But it has come now. The people are singing the pre-sermon hymn, and in a minute they will sit down and look up with expectation . . . and the better they have been fed, the keener is their expectation. But there is a prayer in the preacher's heart, and a text maybe in his mind. Reversing the direction of his Lord's words, but keeping faithfully to their meaning, let him say: 'I did not choose You but You have chosen me and ordained me that I should go and bring forth fruit and that my fruit should remain . . .'

It is a thrilling word. The preacher is ready now. The preparation of the moment links on to the preparation of the day and panels itself into the preparation of the whole life. There is still a mystery about this 'plus of the Spirit', and it will be for ever true that the Spirit bloweth where *He* listeth, but in this three-fold preparation of the life, and the day, and the moment, the obedient servant offers himself unreservedly to God and knows—whether he is used or laid aside—that he can do no more.

THREE

THE HUSBANDRY OF TIME

No man can be a consistently effective preacher who begrudges the time which pulpit preparation takes. The wisest use of his time is one of the major problems with any minister of God.

To begin with, he is largely master of his own time. That is both a privilege and a peril. No one—unless it be the Recording Angel—takes heed of his hour of beginning work, nor with what resolution he goes at it till the day is done. It is not the least of the responsibilities placed upon him by ordination that, in the main, he may order his own life.

There is, moreover, a peculiar dilemma which preachers have to solve in their handling of time. They must be—like King Alfred—'noble misers' of their moments, and yet they must appear to have plenty to spare. They must be more keen than Kipling to see that every minute gives its 'sixty seconds' worth of distance run', and yet they must always be accessible to people: easy to approach and easy to confide in. No one can confide intimate things to a man whose eye keeps wandering to his watch, and whose whole manner makes it clear that he is only giving half his mind.

Furthermore, the trend of modern church life tends to make the minister increasingly a business man. Indeed, some ministers have more letters to write than many people engaged in commerce: more committees to attend than high executives: more visits to pay than doctors in general practice. How to compass that volume of work and yet remain a minister—a man of God whose chief business is to point the path to Heaven and who guards hours of every week for pulpit preparation? If a man becomes an academic recluse, his people lose their pastor, and a man who is no pastor impoverishes his pulpit work as well. If a minister permits the business man within him to harden his nature, he becomes metallic, can only be seen by appointment, and may even be guarded by folk who require a caller to 'state his business'.

How difficult it is, even for a consecrated man, to pick the saddle-path between these precipices: to remain a serious student even if he cannot be an outstanding scholar: to be a man of the world, and not cease to be a man of God: to be dependable in whatever business affairs he must handle, but clearly most dependable in the business of handling souls: to waste no moments, and yet to have all the time there is for any burdened body nigh to heart-break: to meet every legitimate claim his people might make upon him, and yet never mount his pulpit steps inadequately prepared to break the bread of life. Who is sufficient for these things? How can a man be steadily on guard against the sloth of his nature and all these opposing perils of the parson's calling? How can he find, in these competing claims upon his time, those blocks of hours in every week which must be kept sacred for pulpit preparation and without which he cannot be a servant of the Word?

The two chief enemies are laziness and trivial occupation. John Wesley, in his twelve rules for his helpers, pilloried both these enemies in Rule One. 'Be diligent. Never be unemployed. Never be triflingly employed. Never while away time, nor spend more time at any place than is strictly necessary.' There are twenty-four hours in the day of all of us. A labourer works eight. A minister of God cannot do less than twelve. Spurgeon averaged fifteen over many years—but died at fifty-seven of gout and overwork. Twelve is a good average to keep in mind. Some days a little more, and some a little less. But those who have interior peace and know how to relax between jobs, and even (when they are routine tasks) to relax *in* them, will not find twelve hours a day too costing.

It is impossible to set down a 'typical day' in any minister's life because every man's life is different from every other, and every day has its touch of variety even in the same man's life. But to think about it in any reasonable way at all, let us divide it into three parts: the mornings for study; the afternoons for visitation; the evenings for meetings and interviews. Nothing is said here of devotions (the first claim on any man's time); and nothing is said of recreation (though it demands its minor place in our week); and nothing is said of those committees which are not covered by 'evening meetings' or of any evenings given to the counsel of souls. But these rough thirds come nearer to being 'typical' than any other division of a minister's time. It is on those morning hours that I would concentrate in my concern about preaching and the preparation for it. Aim at a minimum of four hours a day of hard mental work. Have a big, well-chosen book always on hand. Don't be a hand-to-mouth preacher, whose whole study in every week is for next Sunday's sermons. Give some of that hard thinking to the upper levels of thought, which will render no obvious return next Sunday but which will give a largeness and strength to all your public utterances in all the years of your active work.

I want to suggest ways in which that precious time can be guarded. We have recognized the dangers we have to meet: our own inertia; our vulnerability to people who would waste our time on trifles; our own indiscipline in not having 'first things first' when we get down to work; the trend of the times, which would place upon the minister of God all kinds of civic and social service, important in their minor way, but cumulatively perilous in their power to steal him from his primary occupation. . . . We are to measure ourselves against these and other dangers. How can we be expert in the husbandry of time?

We must develop *a keen sense of time*. It is a precious gift from God and man. God grants us life, and our fellow-men labour that we may give our whole time to holy things. Poor as our economic status usually is, we are living on the Christian community. Whenever we look at our people and especially when we see, at the Holy Table, toil-worn hands stretched out for the bread and the wine, let us remember that we are living on other men's labour. That solemn recollection should make us the more diligent in our use of all the time we have.

Some men work best in the early morning, and some late at night. No man is wise who attempts both. 'You can't be a lark *and* an owl.' A man must have respect to his own nature and his mould of circumstance, but most people would agree that an early start is better for those who can manage it. John Henry Jowett began his working day all his ministry at 6 a.m. He grew up in a Yorkshire mill town, and the sound of the clogs in the early morning was among his earliest recollections. Work began in the mills at 6 a.m. Jowett felt, as a minister of God, that he could not make a later start himself. To have one's unhurried devotions over and a start made of the day's work before breakfast, adds to the appetite both for the meal and the work. But men vary and some of us achieve more the other way round. The important thing is to get the hours in and the work done.

We must learn also to *distinguish between ten minutes and a quarter-of-an-hour*. The opinion has been expressed by men interested in health and work that, perhaps, no man had a greater output of work in proportion to his health than Charles Darwin. His son, Sir Francis Darwin, explained it in this way. 'A striking characteristic was his respect for time: he never forgot how precious it was. He would often say that saving the minutes was the way to get work done; he showed his love of saving the minutes in the difference he felt between a quarter-of-an-hour and ten minutes' work; he never wasted a few spare minutes from thinking that it was not worth while to set to work. The same eager desire not to lose time was seen in his quick movements when at work.'

If a man were to check his use of time—and made it a religious duty so to do—he would probably be surprised how much time during a whole day had been wasted 'in little bits'. Reading the paper before lunch; sitting over breakfast longer than the meal or courtesy requires; pottering about. Years are short but minutes are long. How much could be done without rush or strain in salvaged minutes!

It would help us also if we learned *how to use travel time*. Most of us spend time in travel: some of us, a great deal of time. If a man is driving a car, he must put his whole mind on driving (and not disgrace the cloth by recklessness or discourtesy on the road!), but, in public transport, he has all his time to think. How wise to have the theme of a spiritual meditation in the ante-chamber of one's mind, so that even on a short journey one can visit the great quietness where God dwells, and come back with the serene tranquillity in which all our work should be done. Or, perhaps, it is a bit of hard thinking on a sermon theme, or a cunning illustration to be fashioned. . . . It is all thinking. The rhythm of wheels aids thought. So much precious time in travel is lost in day-dreaming. Short journeys can be used both for mind and soul.

But *long* train journeys!—what a gift they can be. No telephone to disturb you now. No callers. The carriage becomes your study and your oratory too. Pull down the shutters of your ears against the chatter of the carriage. Alone with God, you can get deep into mental prayer and deep into philosophical thought: a sermon can be outlined: notes for an article you mean to write: the heart torn out of a book: a file of letters dealt with . . . and no rush! Just the quiet economy of moments. Not that you will be indifferent to the chance of a useful conversation as you travel. People sometimes unburden their hearts to ministers in railway carriages, and the journey may prove most valuable in a pastoral way. But the passenger who wants to bore you with the details of his operation ('And the doctor said he had never seen a bigger . . .') must be made to realize that you are busy. He will feel no doubt that the parson 'kept himself to himself', but your smile of farewell will convince him that you were not unfriendly. In any case, your time is not your own.

And that leads me to say: '*Don't covet the distinction of being clubbable.*' I know that runs counter to the advice which many laymen give to young ministers, and counter, also, to the ambition you may have in your heart. It is nice to be known in the neighbourhood as 'matey' and 'a good sort': to be smacked on the back by Tom, Dick, and Harry, and in constant demand at Rotary Clubs, the British Legion, and in other places where men foregather.

But you will buy that distinction dearly. To other losses, you will need to add the loss of precious time. The more you get into these marginal things, the less time you will have at your desk: perhaps, also, at your prayers. The less time at your desk and your prayers, the less power in the pulpit. You are a man of God in the community. Separate! Not by your choosing but by God's choice. That does not mean that you will be aloof and, least of all, superior. God forbid! You are the servant of all. But the community should not know you, first, as 'a good fellow', and then almost remember with surprise that you are a minister of God. But, first, as a minister of God, and other things afterwards if they will.

To this keen sense of the preciousness of time, one must add *skill in dealing with time-wasters*. We have seen that the minister is especially vulnerable to their attention. So important is it that the minister be available to everybody in genuine need, and so important is it that he be easily approachable by the most timid soul, that he is easy game for people with time to waste and with a taste for ministerial company. Every church of any size contains its little group of time-wasters. They invent reasons for bothering a busy man. They are afflicted with circumlocution. Things that could be said in moments take them a quarter of an hour. They haunt the vestry door, the church porch, and the manse. A moment is enough with some of them. A bright word and a handshake sets them on their way. But others are painfully persistent and stronger measures must be used against them.

It is best to let the people know quite frankly, when first coming among them, that, *in their interests,* you must guard your morning hours for study. Let it be clear that, at any time of day or night, you are ready in emergency, but, saving matters of the gravest concern, you would be glad to be left undisturbed by doorbell or telephone before lunch. It is in their service that you are engaged. With God and with your books, you are closeted in preparation for the holy day. The nourishment that you will have for them on Sunday depends on their forbearance in the week.

The great bulk of our people willingly respond to such a word. Indeed, most of them like it. If they are well fed on Sunday, and know their minister is visiting in the afternoons, they are not given to complaining. Our folk are not fools. With all our variety of temperament and human frailty, they know if we are all-out for God and unsparing of ourselves.

Nor, I beg you, undertake pastoral visitation in the morning except, again, in emergency. There are some men who actually believe that 'a home-visiting parson makes a church-attending people', and that church life is a matter of reciprocity in calling on one another. People ought not to be indulged in such shallow thinking, and made to suppose that we go to God's house to return the parson's call. I have known men who so magnified the work of pastoral visitation above all other aspects of their task that they had 'morning lists' for visitation, and called before noon on certain ladies in their congregation who rather enjoyed being on the 'morning list'. Preaching and pastoral work ought never to be thrown into opposition with one another, but, collecting a congregation by constant visitation, and having nothing to set before them when they come, is not a course to commend. If we are careless ourselves in guarding our morning hours for intercourse with God and our deepest thinking, how can we expect our people to realize the awesome importance of what we do?

But what are we to do with those time-wasters whom no frankness about our pre-occupations, and no efforts to evade, can really suppress, and who invade our privacy against all discouragement and hinder our work? We may be glad that the most hardened ones are not numerous, and I can give no help except this:—being sure of my man, and knowing that nothing of importance had brought him and no normal word would get him to go, I have simply given him the chapter, or the sermon, or the article that I was engaged upon when he came. I did my thinking aloud as it were. I beat out my thoughts on his mind. I firmly directed the conversation to those things I had to do, and found that he lost the taste for my company much sooner than if I had indulged in the idle chatter which was the main staple of his talk.

But a wise and firm wife can save a man from much of this—even though she may get disliked herself by doing it. George Morrison's wife earned her husband's deep gratitude by guarding him from the time-wasters, though she did not escape the disfavour of those she kept away. Often she gave her time to save his.

To a sense of the preciousness of time, and firm adroitness with those who would waste it, we must add an unobtrusive *mastery of business method*. I say 'unobtrusive' because it is not a good thing that the major impression a minister gives his people is that he is 'a business man'. But a business man he must be nonetheless.

It belongs to the vanity of some laymen engaged in commerce to suppose that no ministers are business men.

The truth is, of course, that certain ministers are among the ablest business men in the community. There are, indeed, some (as we have hinted) who almost allow the business man to swallow the shepherd of souls, and the more we master such degree of business method as our calling requires, the more we must be on our guard against that danger.

A degree of business method in the ministerial life is a religious duty. It is, after all, only a way of getting necessary work well done and avoiding waste of time. It is 'taking trouble to save trouble'. Exquisite refinements of business method we do not need, but there is a minimum we cannot do without. Lacking that, the work of God suffers.

Some men come into the ministry after business training, and find that training of incalculable use. But others heard the call of God at the tail of a plough, or in an academic hall, or in a mine, and business methods are strange to them. None of us would lose by mastering one good book on office efficiency. Its counsel will need adaptation to the ministerial calling, but this is simply done. Methods which experienced ministers have found of use are willingly shared in staff meetings. Let a man be on his guard against earning a reputation for being forgetful or unbusinesslike (and thinking it funny!) and he will soon learn that tasks done by method and to time, save more hours than they take up.

Here are a few simple bits of counsel. Read your letters once only, and with a pen or pencil in hand. *Underline the things which require answer.* Some of our correspondents are verbose and may even put the real purpose of their writing in a postscript. If the answer is a little involved, write a précis of your reply on the top of the letter. If it calls for decision, make the decision

D

(when possible) right away. Write it on the letter. It will not need reading again.

Make agenda for your days. Don't let the precious time drift away wondering after each job: 'What shall I do next?' I have found it a useful practice to make my agenda a minor part of my devotions. I want my days ordered by God. Planning the day's work with God keeps the 'priorities' right. So work and prayer knit into one another and toil remains 'unsevered from tranquillity'. Diaries which are interleaved with blank pages are most useful. The thought-out and prayed-over agenda set down on the blank page is all the while under one's eye.

Some system of filing papers we must have. Hunting for a letter, or newspaper cutting, in a muddled heap is wasteful of time and fretting to the nerves. It is, as Whittier knew, 'our *ordered* lives' which can confess the beauty of God's peace. We have no time for over-elaborate systems, but a simple, alphabetical, and datal order we must have. Most men will find useful 'the advance file' which brings to our notice every task on the day on which it must be done. The memory ought not to be burdened with routine. Let the 'business method' carry detail. Unfailingly, as we look each day into our advance file, we shall be told what must be done *now*: those returns must all be in: that schedule must go off: the insurances are to be paid. It is bothersome, of course, in some ways, to a man longing to wrestle with a great theme, but it will be more bothersome later if it isn't done. Neglect of these details is sheer selfishness in the end. It gives other people extra trouble and it is not the mark of 'a great mind'.

It is not always easy, in our full lives, to decide what to do now and what to defer. I am not thinking at the moment of the larger 'priorities', concerning which I have more to say presently, but just how to find the balance between the extreme of deferring everything, and the extreme of dropping whatever one is doing at any time to attend to the last (and, perhaps, trivial) call. I have known men overdo both. If a thing is dealt with instantly, it is dealt with. It need not go on the agenda at all. 'I must remember to do that' will not haunt the mind. *It is done.* An agenda must not be so long as to be frightening. Away with this little thing at once.

On the other hand, if, for instance, a man has his mind under way on an important subject, e.g. a sermon theme which has just burst open, and his thoughts are cascading out, he need not and should not leave that instantly because some minor matter of church administration pops up. A note is enough. It will have my mind *some time today*. Right on with the big job.

There is a balance to be found between these extremes and one develops an extra gift for finding it. A sense of time, a skill in dealing with those who waste it, and a quiet mastery of business method, are important preliminaries in this great task of becoming 'noble misers' of our moments. For the rest, I can make my mind still more clear if I group my counsel under three heads. There are things to—

1. Eliminate
2. Delegate
3. Cultivate

Let us look at each of them in turn.

1. *Eliminate.* Don't feel compelled to accept every invitation to speak in public. Any man who has facility with words gets more requests than he can wisely accede to. All kinds of clubs, civic and social gatherings, little

'uplift' societies, press their claims upon him. He cannot
be a recluse and say 'No' to them all, though that would
be less serious than saying 'Yes' to them all. He must
test them in the light of his chief purposes and really
reserve himself for his big task. He is in the community
to offer the gospel of the living God to needy men and
women. Nothing must be allowed seriously to divert
him from that. Let him learn to say 'No' so nicely that
his correspondents feel almost as happy as though he had
said 'Yes'.

Don't read every book pressed upon you by enthu-
siasts, or extravagantly praised by the reviewer who
praises all things. Ministers probably waste more time
over reading than over anything else. Thinking and
praying are our great needs. But what reading we do is
so important that the choice of the big book on hand
ought never to be casual. Learn to sort books: the
derivative book from the source book: the book which
is honestly worth a skim from the book which must be
mastered and précised. If a young man wonders how he
can tell the one from the other, let him begin by learning
who the more dependable book-reviewers are but, better
still, let him send a line to his old professor. A postcard
from a master of the subject will save many wasted hours.

Don't become a book-reviewer yourself—unless you
are well paid for it and badly need the money, and unless
the book's subject is one in which you are (or are beginning to be) a specialist. The custom of 'paying' the
reviewer by letting him keep the book may be generous
payment for a hasty reading and a few innocuous lines
but it is perilous for a conscientious man who undertakes
the work seriously and wastes many precious hours over
books he would otherwise have never read at all. I
calculated, when I had been myself ensnared into this

dangerous course, that I would have read about one in five of the books sent me for review. For the privilege of having on my shelves many books I didn't want, I was ill-using hours and hours of my mental life. I gave it up.

Don't develop a taste for committees. Some service on committees we must all do, because it is in committee that much of the necessary work of the Church is done. Wholesale condemnation of committees is foolish. If committees did not function, the worst evils of bureaucracy, and even autocracy, would be upon us. But some men learn to love them for themselves alone: count it an 'honour' to be on more committees than their neighbour: angle for the 'privilege'. . . . Resist that infection of thought. Every committee must be converted in your mind into so many *less* pastoral calls, so much *less* sheer thought, so much *less* direct work of the ministry. Do your share of this work and no more. Use your influence in committees honestly to do the business but with all the expedition which is possible. Remember that when the committee has passed the resolution, *nothing has been done*. The actual *work* is still to be started.

Time saved is time made. The husbandry of time requires that we be skilful in eliminating the unnecessary.

2. *Delegate*. It is one of the recurrent sins of the Christian Church that she uses many of her best brains on office boy's work. It may prove the humility of her servants that they cheerfully undertake the work, but it is a scandalous waste, nonetheless, and, ultimately, impoverishing to the Church. Men are professionally trained for six or seven years before ordination, and then spend hours of every week in minor routine tasks which a bright child could undertake. Temple Gairdner's biographer reminds her readers that Gairdner was

contemporary at Oxford with F. E. Smith, John Simon, and Hilaire Belloc, and fully their intellectual peer, but she has many occasions to deplore the fact that, when he became a missionary, his fine brain was employed often on trivialities, and she marvels at the misuse of so splendid a mind. Is it possible for the minister to delegate some of his work . . . and how?

There are tasks which, by their very pastoral privacy, only the minister himself can do. They belong to his office as such. No thought of their delegation ever crosses his mind. But there are other tasks which can be farmed out. The filing of letters and newspaper-cuttings: the distribution of magazines: the summoning of meetings through the post: routine correspondence: duplication . . . what a vast amount of time can go on tasks like these. A man of business method will economize his moments even here, but the man who can delegate the whole lot saves even more time.

Resist the vanity of supposing that a thing isn't done well unless you do it yourself. In all churches of any size there are people eager to work for God. Some of them have no gift in public speech but they have other gifts. They would appreciate the opportunity to help. Convinced that their minister is fully extended in God's service, they would love to lift burdens from him that he might the more assiduously do what he alone can do. Why not use those people? It is part of a minister's task to see a gift in a man or woman which they have not seen themselves. Quiet, discreet, unobtrusive but effective help, rendered to a minister behind the scenes, can give him precious additional hours in every week the more faithfully to do the direct work of God. Some of the delegated tasks may not be done *quite* so well as you would have done them. Does that matter—if they are routine tasks? Take eighty per cent as one hundred per cent in all delegated work. Choose your helpers wisely and trust them firmly, and all will be the gainers in the end.

If your church does not provide secretarial help—and few do—get it yourself. It can be part-time help at first. A shorthand-typist may be eager to make a little extra money. A person in training for secretarial service may be seeking beginner's experience. In the time you save in that way an article can be written which will pay the cost of the help for a couple of weeks. Or an excessive smoker could cut his tobacco to a fraction and add to his efficiency and his health at the same time. It is not enough to be busy. Our business is to be busy on the best things, and every task which can be delegated means more time for those tasks which only we can do.

3. *Cultivate*. No minister has ever really 'done' his work. There is no moment when he can sit down and feel that there is no job on the desk, no people to visit, and nothing to pray over. It is only in a relative sense that he can keep abreast of his work.

What he specially needs to cultivate is a sense of the essential: how to have his 'priorities' right: in what order to take the tasks which clamour simultaneously for attention and, when he ends a hard day with something undone, to have the comfortable assurance that the unfinished tasks are the least important. As I have hinted, many men are tearingly busy on un- or less essential things. Only as a man lives in the light of God, with a clear understanding of what his chief business is, will he have any deftness in putting his work in order of priority. Some of the less important parts of our work scream the loudest. If a man will give his freshest mind to praying, and the 'square block' of his morning hours to his hardest mental work, it will surprise him how many of the lighter tasks can be slipped into the salvaged half-hours of the rest of his day. Men who make a rule of clearing up all minor business items immediately after breakfast, intending to turn with a fresh mind to deeper things later, often find that the deeper things don't get a fresh mind at all.

Separated to holy things: a preacher of the word: a pastor of the people . . . these ruling convictions in his mind will do more than a little to select the tasks which must come first.

One other ruling thought will help to keep our 'priorities' right. Few of us work quite alone. Most of us are blessed with colleagues. It sometimes happens that others cannot get forward with their work unless we speedily attend to certain things first. Some priority should be given to tasks which, left undone, hinder the work of others similarly employed for God, and similarly impressed with the desire to have 'first things first'.

But when, at the end of a full day, we are 'oppressed by things undone' (even though they be the least important things), let there be no worry or inward fret. Hand the day quietly over to God as one who has done his best, and go to sleep.

Going to sleep—for those who are living a very full life—is another thing to cultivate, and not at night only. The art of snatch-sleeping is a skill busy men need to acquire, especially in the middle years. I am not thinking of those who fall to sleep involuntarily (sometimes, even when we are preaching!), but the power to sleep *at will*, and wake, within minutes, refreshed. Men of great achievement in all walks of life have cultivated this gift: Wesley, Wellington, Napoleon, Gladstone, Clifford. . . . It was a priceless boon to them. Dr. F. Luke Wiseman told me once that he had so cultivated this gift in his full life that, often dining alone in an hotel, he would sleep between the courses. A man, no longer young, working ten or twelve hours a day, would find his output increased if he learned the art of complete relaxation and taught himself to summon sleep whenever he wished. Ten minutes in a train or vestry can work wonders. Complete relaxation is beneficial even if sleep does not come. To take the tension out of the whole body—even the crease out of the preacher's tongue!—and come back serenely fresh again, is worth untold wealth to those who work almost all the hours they are awake.

Finally, I would urge you to guard a reasonable period of recreation, if you are living (as you ought to be) a full life. If it can be in the open air, so much the better. It is not time wasted. We owe it to God and to our people to keep fit. If sickness overtakes us, it ought not to be by our folly or implicit consent. The temple of the Holy Ghost should be as worthy of its Divine Resident as we can make it, and we shall save more time than we lose by giving the body its due, and 'thinking health'.

So—in all these things—shall we be good husbandmen of our time, seeking, saving, 'making' that precious commodity, that we may, above all else, do the work to which we are called.

FOUR

THE CONDUCT OF WORSHIP

GONE are the days when everything preceding the sermon in Free Church worship was called 'the preliminaries'. Perhaps the word or idea was never as common as our critics have suggested. God has never left us without our quiet saints and they, of all people, would never have dismissed the prayer, and praise, and Bible Reading as hors-d'oeuvre to the exposition. Yet it is a fact that so much emphasis was put upon the preaching among us that the preciousness of other parts of worship was sometimes obscured, and it is still as common in Free Church services to hear the officiating minister described as the 'preacher' as to hear it said that 'the Rev. A. B. will conduct worship'.

Moreover, the form of divine service most commonly used in the Free Churches has come under sharp criticism for a generation past. Some of the severest critics have been Free Churchmen themselves. Divine worship, on this model, is said to be a loose sequence of unrelated items. The service is said to lack wholeness and unity. Extempore prayer, it is affirmed, is unhelpful to many, and even repulsive to a few. Some Free Churches have adopted semi-liturgical forms of worship, and not many who write on these subjects seem eager to defend the old simplicities of the dissenting way.

I want to plead for the free form of worship. Those who put weight upon the practice of the Early Church will welcome the reminder that non-liturgical worship is the older way. Justin Martyr and Tertullian leave one in no doubt about that. There was no full development of a fixed liturgy in the first three centuries of the Church.

But it is not so much ancient practice as modern need which will weigh with most of us. We are less impressed with the customs of the early saints than with the service of the later sinners. Vast multitudes of our fellow-countrymen are estranged from the Church. They are not theoretical atheists. Some segment of their heart still holds out for God. Occasionally they come to worship. By the hunger of their heart, or the constraint of a friend, they are drawn in, and may be drawn in increasingly in coming years. I am convinced that the free form of service gives us the best opportunity with them. The non- or irregular church-goer is confused by liturgy. He fumbles with an unfamiliar book. What is so simple to the regular worshipper is complicated to him, and, if he lacks great persistence, he slips out easily again. If the worship is not merely liturgical but highly ritualistic, his confusion is worse confounded. I was praying alone one day, in the course of my pastoral visitation, in an Anglo-Catholic church in a poor part of London and found myself in conversation afterwards with the deaconess. She mistook my kind of churchmanship. 'No, Father!' she said. 'Nobody from the neighbourhood comes to worship here. I visit and invite them, but they say they can't understand when they come. . . .'

Ought worship to be so incomprehensible as that? Surely, even prodigals should feel at home when they are there? Is the only way back by a long corridor labelled 'catechumenate'? Should it be?

The free form of worship is not a poor kind of worship, though it has been poorly used and sadly misused. The extra freedom it gives to the minister has not always been well taken but, in itself, it is flexible: able to express every aspect of worship, and capable of bringing home to people the awe-ful sense of God. Because it requires more of the minister, the conduct of Divine service should be the most serious study of all who lead in non-liturgical worship. If men—whose high duty in leading public praise consists in the reverent reading of ancient and familiar prayers—should bring to their service the zest which liturgiologists display, how much more should those men be zealous who may and must shape the act of worship on each Sabbath as it comes and bear to God in their own words the adoration, confession, thanksgiving, and intercession of the people. The conduct of worship in Free Churches is a task so responsible that any man might well shrink from it. There is point in the contention of those people who argue that *too* much is left to the minister, and that his personal convictions, his moods, and even his prejudices, are in danger of obtruding at the mercy seat. The danger must be admitted—and overcome. The answer to all this is not a flight to liturgies but a solemn re-consecration to the hard task laid upon us by our office and ordination, and an iron resolve before God to do this solemn work well. I want us to consider ways in which we may do it well —admitting, as we begin, that even small things are large if they either help or hinder people in their access to God.

Is a man's attire, when he conducts worship, too trivial for mention? On the condition that we have laid down, that nothing is too small for notice if it is an impediment to those who come seeking the Father, it clearly calls for passing reference. No custom of general observance yet prevails in all the Free Churches concerning the attire of those who conduct worship. One wishes, in some ways, that it did. Time was when a clerical frock-coat would be seen in any pulpit occupied by a minister, but fashion and austerity have almost banished clerical frock-coats. Lounge suits—unhappily—have largely taken their place, and they are not always black and they are not always pressed. The ill-grooming of some men in the pulpit is a disgrace to their office. To tilt against an over-emphasis on ecclesiastical vestments, and then come to the solemn leading of worship without that scrupulous cleanliness, neatness and freshness which is possible to the poorest among us, is quite unworthy. The supposition that this slovenliness is the mark of a great or scholarly mind adds vanity to irreverence. There is a way of worshipping God in our dress. It is as free from ostentation as from carelessness. Deny it as some folk will, it is a fact that people are helped by the fresh and healthy appearance of their minister. If one cannot always be fit and look fit, one should aim to. The disappearance of the clerical frock-coat has meant an increase in the use of a preaching gown in the pulpit. There are small groups of people here and there who seem to regard the gown as 'popish', and one has no desire to offend folk over minor matters, but still more congregations regard the dress as seemly, and not a few prefer their minister attired, in the manner of John Wesley, with gown and cassock and bands.

If dress is a matter of some small importance, so also is deportment, and for the same reason. Utter disregard of it does not conduce to worship. The idea of a minister taking a course in deportment might be mildly amusing, and to be self-conscious about one's bearing would almost certainly defeat one's end, but there is a manner which is seemly and a manner which is not. It is not fitting for a man to rush into a pulpit, or 'balloon' into it, or sneak into it. It is not fitting for a man to sprawl across his pulpit desk, or stand with his hands in his pockets, or loll about. Rightly or wrongly, it gives the impression that the man himself has not come from the audience chamber of Heaven with a message from God, and that he has no sense of his ambassadorial status. And if the minister—though all unworthy—does not feel a messenger of God himself, what hope that the people will feel it of him?

Some men, when they are leading worship, leave the impression that they are not joining in the worship themselves. They stand, and hand it out to the people. 'Here is a hymn for you to sing. When you've done that, I'll give you something more.' They do not sing themselves, and that would not be serious because a man may want to rest his voice and listen, but they have a strange air of detachment the whole time.

Young ministers inquire sometimes whether they ought to employ gestures in the conduct of worship and of preaching. A course in how to gesticulate is more amusing than a course in deportment. The fact is that gesticulation is a natural expression of some personalities and not of others. Some of us cannot speak at any length without using our hands. If we were handcuffed, we should be dumb! Others feel no impulse to gesticulate at all. Archbishop William Temple could speak for a gripping hour without a gesture. Be yourself! If gesture is natural, see that it is not excessive and not ugly. Success in the service is measured by the increasing degree in which the minister fades from the people's mind 'and God is all in all'.

Should the order of service always be the same order? Not always!—and yet not too frequently or too completely changed. The means of expression in worship are

not infinite. Adoration, thanksgiving, confession, intercession, petition, and dedication on the manward side,
and forgiveness, guidance, counsel, and comfort on the
Godward side, have all to appear somewhere, either in
hymns, music, prayer, Bible reading, preaching or
silence. The variations of order in these vehicles of
expression are not numerous. Avoiding an imprisoning
rigidity of order on the one hand, and a capricious
changefulness (which would leave the people quite
uncertain where they are) on the other, the minister can
shape the act of divine worship so that it shall bear this
solemn commerce of earth and heaven.

Certainly, the service should have wholeness. Every
legitimate element of worship should be present. The
service has not failed if 'the people do not have a good
sing' (though more than one completely new tune is too
many!), but if adoration, thanksgiving, confession, or
intercession has been omitted, it has failed to be a complete act of worship. A minister planning the service
must see it *whole*. He is a legitimate object of criticism
if he throws it together without seeking for a worshipful
completeness. Four hymns chosen just because the people
like them (they might all be songs sung to one another
and not addressed to God at all!). One Bible reading
chosen because it is the context of the word the preacher
means to expound and the other cut out to allow time
for a children's address! One prayer purely invocative,
and the other (which ought not in wisdom be *long*)
touching on a few particularized ideas! . . . This is not
using the free form of worship with understanding and
seriousness. The charge of 'unrelated items' is fully
proven here. It is even possible that some who have
been guilty of this blasphemous bowdlerizing were
unaware of their own crassness. No wonder this form of

worship has been criticized if many who use it, use it so ill.

Nor do all those people help who press for 'unity' in the service without reaching for the larger unity we need. Some there are who plan the service too narrowly: who secure unity by the sacrifice of comprehension. Thanksgiving, maybe, is in their mind. The whole service is thanksgiving. Hymns, prayer, Bible reading, sermon— all thanksgiving! It is unity—but at what a price! The prodigal turning his eyes home again has no offer of forgiveness. The man sentenced to death by the doctor two days before feels the whole service strangely remote. The woman who has found out that her husband is philandering with someone else finds it all going over her head. . . . No one service can deal fully with the whole gamut of human need, but every service should include the main elements which constitute worship and reach towards completeness in this contact with Heaven. There is a structure in a service which anyone responsible for conducting worship will ignore only at the people's loss. When the structure is fashioned to its highest use, all the parts contribute to the richness of the whole.

With the wholeness of the service ever in mind, how is it best to begin?—with a call to worship, silent prayer, vocal prayer, a hymn, or an introit? A case can be made out for each of these ways of beginning. Perhaps different openings can be used at different times. A call to worship —in scriptural or non-scriptural language—puts the people in mind at once of the solemn purpose of meeting: to invite them to be utterly silent in the presence of God secures the same end: if one begins with a hymn, the call can immediately precede it, and the hymn could either be a hymn of praise and thanksgiving to God, a call to salvation, or an invitation to one's fellow-worshippers to join in adoration.

Music can be very enriching to Divine worship—and very hindering, too. Happy is the minister whose organist is his whole-souled colleague and whose choir is both technically good and spiritually keen. A choir which is poor in either of these particulars is best dispensed with. If the choir is petty and quarrelsome, it will inject disharmony into the church. If it cannot sing well, it is best to dispense with introits and anthems. The idea that 'we ought to let the choir have a turn' borders on the profane. The hurt given to really musical people in the congregation by the screeching efforts of incompetent choirs is a form of cruelty which ought not to be indulged. The standard of musical appreciation among our people is rising rapidly. The best of broadcast music accounts for that. Not even the pious recollection of the congregation that the poor choir has done its best, fully restores them to the spirit of worship when blissful silence supervenes upon an awful blast of 'song'. And, as to allowing a choir of this calibre to open the service with an introit . . . well, it is offensive to man and barely redeemed by its sincerity to God. A poor choir can still render a useful service in public worship by leading the congregational singing, and it should not be allowed to do more than that. And this, after all, is the chief duty of a church choir at any time.

The choice of *hymns* is a matter of major importance. We have already noted that only some hymns are addressed to God. The others are addressed to fellow-worshippers (e.g. 'Fight the good fight'; 'Come, let us all unite and sing'; 'Come, let us with our Lord arise'), or to our own soul (e.g. 'Come, my soul, thy suit prepare'; 'Awake, my soul, and with the sun'). Some

E

students would use the word 'hymn' only for those
spiritual songs which are addressed to the Deity, but
common usage employs the word in the wider way.
The important thing is that the minister be clear about
the difference himself. Both kinds of hymn have their
use but, clearly, only one kind can be direct adoration,
confession, intercession, and prayer.

In many Free Churches, the hymn-book is a prayer-
book. Not all the hymns were intended for public singing. Some are there for personal meditation and private
devotion. Others are intended for public use but only on
rare occasions and, one supposes, for select and specially
prepared companies (e.g. 'Come, Saviour, Jesus, from
above'; 'Holy Spirit, pity me'). To know his hymn-
book thoroughly should be the aim of every man who
uses the free form of service: to know its highways and
byways: to put his finger swiftly on *just* the hymn he
wants: to know enough about tunes to converse intelli-
gently with his organist and choir master about them: to
find a balance and range in his choice at every service. . . .

Services can almost be killed by the wrong hymns.
Some men are guilty of choosing long hymns with
ponderous metres for their first two hymns, infusing that
awful sense of 'drag' into a service before it has barely
begun. They seem to know nothing of the craft of
getting swiftly into a service without the slightest sense
of rush or loss of dignity. A burst of praise to begin. . . .
A wondering, adoring invocation to the Blessed God
already there. . . . The Lord's Prayer and a gentle hymn,
addressed, perhaps, to the Holy Spirit . . . and here we
are, with our heads already in the Book of God and
hanging on the timeless words of Holy Scripture. . . .
('Isn't it good to be here!' the people are thinking, and,
indeed, it is.)

The range and richness of the hymn-book, and the important place of the hymns in worship, can be brought out by the minister in a phrase or two when announcing the hymn: 'Let us confess our failings to God as we sing . . .'; 'We will cheer each other on our pilgrim way with the hymn . . .'; 'The hymn number. . . . It is a prayer to the Holy Spirit.' The wealth of devotion in a rich hymnology—one thinks especially of the hymns of Charles Wesley and Isaac Watts—surpasses all our powers of computation. It has been well said that not even the Roman Missal, or the lovely Book of Common Prayer, can surpass a rich hymnology for spiritual nourishment. To know the range and resources of the book oneself, and sharpen the appetite of the congregation for such food, is the privilege of those called of God to lead the worship of His people.

Seldom should more than two hymns in a service be dictated by the sermon theme: one to prepare for it, and one after to give a fitting vent to the hearts and minds of people impressed by that particular truth. The second is more important. It is, perhaps, the only one which should closely match the theme. It is worth almost any effort to achieve the best possible choice for the last hymn.

People who make a slavish rule of *always* reading one line when they announce a hymn, or *always* one verse, are wrong. That calls for no slavish rule. An alert organist doesn't need a rigid rule either. Let the sense and the moment decide it—but let it be real.

To lead in *prayer* is the hardest part of public worship. The 'costing' part of the free form of service is mostly here. Dr. Alexander Whyte called public prayer once 'an unnatural act'—and we know what he meant. Prayer is normally so private: 'God and my soul.' *To pray aloud—and in public!* I do not wonder that some people who can give excellent religious addresses decline to lead in public prayer. Only constant practice could have conquered the embarrassment in anyone of us.

When Earl Baldwin's niece 'leapt over the wall' and left her convent after twenty-eight years of enclosure, she fell in, during one of her many difficulties, with two fine evangelical Christians. She said afterwards that they were far better women than she was ever likely to be, but what staggered her most was their prayers. At the end of a tired day 'these surprising women knelt down like two children at their mother's knee and started to say their prayers. *Out loud*'.

> *It seems incredible, but they really did it. And though I was curiously embarrassed, to them it was the most natural thing in the world. They talked to God exactly as if they saw Him there before them, and knew for a fact that He cared tremendously about their smallest concerns. . . .*
>
> *I quite realize that the idea of such proceedings will give rise to nausea in the stomach of a certain kind of person. . . .*[1]

Twenty-eight years in a convent and staggered by free and intimate prayer! Do we believe deeply in this way of praying? Do we believe in it, not only with two's and three's, but with the great assembly? By what means can we sustain this heaviest part of our holy toil?

There are three honoured traditions of corporate prayer: silent prayer—as exemplified by the Society of Friends: read prayer—used by all who love liturgies: free prayer—which we are discussing now. Each has its difficulties and each its strength. No communion need confine itself rigidly to one manner of praying. The more frequent use of all methods by all believers will

[1] Monica Baldwin, *I Leap Over the Wall*, p. 106 (Hamish Hamilton).

foster that closer fellowship and deeper understanding which nearly all desire. Mind-wandering is a greater problem in silent prayer than in vocalized prayer, though, when it is conquered, this method of praying is unspeakably rewarding in its inner communion. When one is really 'there', one does not want to speak—or not much: one is dumb with wonder, and 'praise sits silent on our tongues'.

Read prayers can have a dignity, and beauty, and proper generality which words immediately summoned can seldom possess. They seem also to soak up the devotion of the centuries and link the generations in 'one blest chain of loving rite'. Yet—especially when they are cast into an imposed order—they can be imprisoning, inflexible, and nobly monotonous.

Free prayer is sensitive to every movement of the Spirit. It can express today's needs today. It can become particular (even though that is one of its perils!), and it sits close to life. It has spontaneity, freedom, and pliancy. On the other hand, it makes immense demands on those who offer it: *spiritual* demands. It requires that a man *abide* under the shadow of the Almighty. It calls for a degree of recollectedness in God's presence which can be achieved in this whirling world only with iron discipline. It can easily degenerate into a succession of trite, outworn phrases just as familiar as the phrasing of ancient liturgy and far less beautiful.

But no one in the Free Church tradition would wish this form of public prayer abandoned. If more use is being made in Free Churches of liturgical forms, no one would wish that the gift of free prayer be lost. A recognition of its difficulties should only quicken us to master them. The idea of a man of God being unable to pray in public without a book is a repellent one to all who are in the Reformed tradition.

The open secret is, of course, in the preparation, not of the prayers, but of oneself. Public prayer is a priestly act. One is going to God *for* the people. That is why a minister must forethink his prayers—not to fix phrasing but to fix a line or a theme. Certain elements must be present in the service (as we have seen) if worship is to have wholeness. One can adore, confess, intercede, and give thanks in hymns, but, where these elements have not been present in the psalmody or the lessons, they must be present in the vocalized prayer. Let a man see his people in imagination before he sees them in the pews: let him think on their wide variety of need: let him identify himself with their fears, sorrows, struggles, triumphs: let him have an order and progression in his thinking (lest he appear in praying to hop about at all odd angles and even grope for something to say next), and let him have, above all else, a sense of wonder that God will and does converse with men at all, and then he will pray acceptably to God and not unhelpfully for men.

And when he feels quite unequal to this hardest part of his vocation, let him remember that even though we know not how to pray as we ought, the Spirit also helps our infirmity and makes intercession for us.

Dr. A. J. Gossip, writing of Professor A. B. Davidson, the distinguished Old Testament scholar, said that his prayers were more mightily moving even than his sermons and lectures.

Always he began with confession. And so terrible was sin to his clean mind; and so near and real and holy was God felt by him to be, there beside him, that his face flushed with the shame of it, and his head sank lower and lower, and his voice faltered and trembled, often broke. And then he would clutch at one or other of the promises,

*and gradually pull himself out of these deep waters, and
back into the sunshine. And by and by his head went up,
and his voice rose in triumph, and the prayer ended in
exultant adoration of a faithful God, who had once more
done exceeding abundantly. . . .*[1]

A minister, whose private devotions include the use
of lovely ancient prayers, and who is soaked in the Scriptures will find that, without any effort, the language meet
in mortals in conversing with their God will rise spon-
taneously to his lips. He will not weary the people with
the constant repetition of the Divine name: he will not
employ sugary expressions in addressing God ('Sweetest
Jesu', etc.—*à la* Stainer's *Crucifixion*): he will not *preach*
in praying—talking obliquely to the congregation instead
of to God: he will not strain for eloquence or hector the
Almighty: he will not work up a spurious fervour or
pray too long: his language will be ever simple and
reverent: never coarse or too familiar: reality will be
written over all this heavenly intercourse and the people
will know that they have talked with God.

Two things will help a man troubled at the thought
that his pulpit prayers are so 'same'. Let him think more
on the wide variety of human need, and think concretely.
Let him think on those who need and deserve our prayers
but are seldom mentioned—e.g. nurses in mental hos-
pitals, officers in approved schools, day-school teachers,
the children of divorcees, missionaries who have con-
tracted leprosy (though that name for the disease is now
banned), the parents of imbecile children, the girl whose
sweetheart was killed in the war, those who fight cruelty
to animals, the woman who fears cancer, the widower,

[1] A. J. Gossip, *In The Secret Place of The Most High*, p. 107 (T. and
T. Clark).

the people marking sad anniversaries in their life . . . the needs are legion. It does much to quicken the spirit of prayer in our people if, in the general pattern of our praying (which *must* have a certain constancy), we add, week by week, one of these particular requests. In six months, a vast range of need is covered: blessing is bespoken on multitudes who require it, and the gamut of our people's sympathy and private praying widely extended too.

If—to this constant survey of the field of need—a man were to approach his self-preparation for prayer with a *theme* in mind, he would often find continuity in an unfolding metaphor. It is spring, maybe, and the preacher sees the daffodils appearing. 'Thanks be to God for spring—His annual revival in nature! Can it be spring-time in our souls? May we feel the stirring of new life within us, the hard but fecund earth broken up again? Is it possible that the breezes of the Holy Spirit may blow about us and new flowers appear in the garden of our soul . . .?'

Or one may see life as a journey across a wide ocean and bear many varied needs to God in a metaphor which is never strained, never obtruded, but which gives a sequence even while it permits diversity.

Invocations are not so hard. The pattern of the collect can serve for many of them. If it is extraordinarily difficult to make a perfect collect, it is comparatively easy to understand its structure and not hard to make an invocation on that model. It opens with the Divine Name drawn out to one aspect of the Divine Nature. It subsumes beneath that aspect of the Divine Nature a particular need, commonly shared, and covered by the ascription already made. It humbly petitions for that precise thing . . . and concludes. Its brevity is not its least merit. One must pray at length at times—but not at *great* length in public.

More men can preach well than can pray well. But the free form of worship will not renew itself until we claim again 'the gift of prayer'.

Bible reading offers the widest scope for the enrichment of public worship and it is a great pity that the Scriptures are often so badly read. Half a lifetime of study has made many preachers familiar with the highways and byways of the Book, and familiar also with the historical background of the component parts, but they forget how strange much of it is to people who must needs spend most of their week labouring for 'the bread which perisheth' and who are quite incapable of setting the particular lesson for the day into its era and circumstance.

Yet, the importance of the Book is quite beyond human computation. It is the word of God in a unique sense. It is not the first book in a class: it occupies a category alone. When the Book is well read and made to live for the people, it can do for them what sermons often fail to do: it can be the very voice of God to their souls. If it fails to be that, the reason is usually to be sought in the lack of high seriousness with which many men come to the task. Their whole manner suggests that anyone can read the Scriptures in public: even a child. The people listen with respect but with only a tithe of that understanding or, indeed, tingling eagerness which skilful readers can communicate to a congregation.

Spurgeon made the Scriptures live for his people by commenting on the verses as he read. Sometimes, however, he grew very wordy and came near to boring the congregation and, if the method proved dangerous with so able an expositor as Spurgeon, it is not surprising that it can become dreadfully tedious with his imitators.

The harder, better way is for a man to read his lessons quietly over in private and, putting himself, in imagination, in the pew as a plumber, or a business man, or a doctor, ask himself if this cutting from the Scriptures would be fully intelligible to him if it were read just as it stands. Sometimes the answer will be 'Yes'. Sometimes the passage will require a title ('A Psalm of Thanksgiving'; 'The Death of Moses'; 'The Call of Samuel'). But quite often the passage will require two or three prefatory sentences to give the people the setting, or the viewpoint, without which full understanding of the Scriptures is not possible. Real skill is called for in shaping those sentences. They must be few and short. They can seldom be cast off without previous reflection. But, done well, and done regularly, and followed by first-class reading, they can be wonderfully enriching to the people.[1] The reading of the Scriptures becomes, by this means, a very high moment in public worship—as, indeed, it ought to be.

Beautiful speaking voices are rare—much rarer, I think, than beautiful singing voices. Nor can one do much about the actual timbre of one's voice: it is given, for good or ill. What one *can* do is, of course, to make the best of what one has and, for most of us, there is a good deal of scope here. Our voice may not be beautiful but—unless we are grievously afflicted—it can be audible, clear, and a most dependable medium for conveying meaning. Indeed, its lack of beauty may even serve our greater ends because there will be no temptation on anybody's part to admire our tonal qualities and less excuse if they do not heed only what we say.

If, to care about audibility and clearness, we are at

[1] See Rupert E. Davies, *Reading Your Bible* (Epworth Press), where the method is illustrated.

pains to correct any faulty pronunciations we may have acquired, and learn what can be taught about the flexibility of the voice, the wise use of range, variety of pace in reading, the power of pause, and the different ways in which emphasis can be achieved . . . we are well on the way to being good readers of the Scriptures. The extremes to avoid are slovenliness on the one hand, and exaggerated elocution on the other. It is not possible to read the Scriptures aloud in a large and echoing church just as one would read them in a drawing-room. More articulation is called for: more pause: more precision. But if this goes beyond a certain point and the Scriptures are 'elocuted' rather than read, it jars the people. The higher skill is to have all the skill hidden. Success is marked by the eagerness of the people for the Scripture Readings in worship—not in acquiring a reputation for being a good reader.

It was my privilege for a few years to be a neighbour of Dr. F. Luke Wiseman. The same stick of bombs which tore off the back of his house tore off my roof, wrecked the garage, and made one vast bomb-hole of the garden. But the walls of my home were still standing and Dr. Wiseman crawled from the débris of his house and took refuge in mine. I was away in a public shelter caring for the bombed-out people at the time, but I hurried over on receiving a message and found the grand old man waiting in the grey dawn. He showed me the bomb-crater in my garden—big enough to take a London bus—and then struck up the old hymn:

> *And are we yet alive,*
> *And see each other's face?*
> *Glory and praise to Jesus give*
> *For His redeeming grace!*

Eighty-two years of age. A bell-like, resonant voice. Unruffled by it all.

But it was Saturday. He was preaching, of course, the next day. The sermons were ready, I gathered, but not the lessons. Had I a Hebrew Bible and a Greek Testament at hand? He settled himself on a dusty settee and began a careful study of his passages. Then he went over them in English. 'It has been my practice to do this,' he said, 'for many years. I like to make the Scriptures live. . . .'

How much he made them live a vast multitude would bear the most willing testimony. You could go home satisfied after he had read the Scriptures—though no one ever did. It was a meal in itself. I fancy I hear him now. He knew the passage well enough to look the people in the face half the time. How skilfully he seemed to throw away whole phrases in order to hover over others! What a difference between his reading of narrative and dialogue. How he ran on there, and dawdled here . . . and the people almost sighed as he finished because his lessons were always too short.

Should one always read the lessons given in the lectionary, or make one's own choice? Completely to ignore the lectionary is to leave whole areas of the Scriptures unread. Rigidly to adhere to the lectionary robs you, on occasion, of a 'background' to the sermon and tends to treat all parts of Scripture as of equal helpfulness. A man must find his own way. Normally, I take one lectionary lesson and one of my own choice— usually germane to the sermon theme though not necessarily containing the text. The really important thing is to come to this task with preparation and high seriousness. Few occupations give a richer return for the time it takes.

It is a criticism of some forms of worship—both

liturgical and free—that they give no time to *silence* in the service: no moments of unhurried waiting on God, with no human voice and no organ heard at all. The criticism is just. Many who come to worship are leading rushing, fevered lives and there are few things they require more than to be utterly quiet.

Yet people need at least a little instruction in the use of corporate silence. It can be oppressive to the uninitiated. They get foolishly tense, do not know how to employ the quietness, and wait impatiently for the end.

Let a minister teach his people how to use the quiet. Let him nourish in them the listening side of prayer. Let him set out before them the varied use the time allows—meditation, mental prayer, openness to the counsel of God . . . and he will find that the period of silence can be lengthened far beyond his early expectations for their appetite will now be truly keen.

Notices can be a nuisance in a service. One must aim to prevent any sense of irritation, but it is disturbing at the heart of solemn worship to read out a succession of minor meetings, many of which, maybe, are far more social than spiritual—a 'hot-pot supper', a 'knife-and-fork tea', a 'one-act play', a 'Krazy Karnival' to mention four which, as a visiting preacher, I have been (expected recently) to give out.

Some large churches seek to escape this embarrassment by having the announcements printed, but always somebody wants something 'stressed'. There is no complete escape from 'notices' in normal worship. Let them be as few, and as short, and as clear as possible.

The custom of dedicating the *offertory* has become common of recent years in the Free Churches. It gathers up, what was once merely a 'collection', into the reverence and dignity of worship. Better so! It brings home to the people that it is to God that the offering is made and quickens their generosities. There are deep ways in which worship is incomplete without 'gift'.

Pronounce the *Benediction*. Do not make an invocation of it. Not '*May* the grace of the Lord Jesus Christ . . .' but 'The Grace of the Lord Jesus Christ. . . .' Pronounce it!

And do not embroider it. The Bible provides us with half-a-dozen glorious benedictions and not one of them can we improve. It is not helpful to hear a man interlarding the words of Holy Scripture with words of his own choosing. 'The grace of the Lord Jesus Christ, and the *precious* love of God, and the *sweet* communion of the Holy Spirit. . . .'

No! no! You cannot improve the Scriptures. A man may prefer to say 'Holy Spirit' for 'Holy Ghost', and he is not unscriptural there, but that should be the limit of his redaction.

Abolish *vespers*—not, of course, by a ministerial fiat but by teaching the people that they are always unnecessary. Often they are banal too. The Benediction is an ultimate. After the grace of the Lord Jesus Christ, and the love of God, and the fellowship of the Holy Spirit, there is nothing that can be added. Nothing! Let the people steal away with the organ sustaining the after-glow of praise.

But for the choir to rise when the Benediction has been pronounced and sing, 'Lord, keep us safe this night', is bathos—and not the less bathetic because they mean well.

Nothing after the Benediction.

Nothing.

FIVE

THE PREACHER AS PASTOR

I

MOST discerning commentators on the ministerial life agree that the offices of preacher and pastor cannot be divorced. It is true that some men have had a pulpit ministry of high effectiveness without going as pastors from door to door, and that many lay preachers exercise no pastoral ministry at all. There is a comment to be made on both these exceptions. It often happens that the minister whose circumstances do not allow him to exercise a full ministry of pastoral visitation is shepherding his people in other ways, and drawing also on a deep experience of home-contacts gathered in other days. It is true, also, that the ministry of the lay preacher would be greatly enriched if he seized opportunities of pastoral oversight and, being appointed to preach, say, in a village church, went out before the hour of service and saw the people in their homes. A preacher must know *people*. No amount of mastery of books can make up for not knowing people. One of the elements in powerful preaching is the skill some men possess to leave people feeling that they have wandered through them with a lighted candle. 'He showed me all my heart.' Often it is done by an aside: a passing reference: an overtone. . . . But all life seems open to such a preacher. The swelling passions of youth: the secret rationalizations of sin: the fingering of evil: the fear of the future: the fight against cynicism: the polluted springs of action . . . he knows it all. How? From his own nature, no doubt, but, also, from his uncommon knowledge of people. Who receives more confidences from men and women? To whom do people more completely unveil themselves? Whose eye is fixed most frequently on that microscope which magnifies our secret motives? The man who has walked the hospital of souls.

Laymen think that ministers are out of touch with life. Some business men—otherwise intelligent—have only the vaguest ideas of what is meant by 'pastoral work', and even suppose that it amounts to nothing more than an afternoon tour by the parson to drink cups of tea with the women of the congregation while their husbands are at the office or the bench. God forgive us that pastoral work has, sometimes, degenerated to that level.

It would be hard to exaggerate the range and depth of pastoral work properly understood. I fell in one day with a ministerial friend who combined a prison chaplaincy with the care of a vigorous church, and he hinted at some of the tasks he had been busy on that week. He had a man in the condemned cell whom he was visiting daily through the dreadful period of waiting: he had been to the juvenile court to say a word for a lad convicted of pilfering: he was cheered that he had at last succeeded in getting a pension for an all-but-blind woman in his church: he had officiated at two funerals.

My own pastoral work that week had covered a fairly wide range. I had seen, by arrangement, three poor sexual perverts who wondered if there was any help for them in religion: I had—at the request of the family—broken the news to an illegitimate boy of the truth of his parentage: I had struggled for hours with a man and woman on the edge of divorce and persuaded them to try again: I had told a man that his wife had inoperable cancer.

As I pondered on the varied duties the week had brought to my friend and to me, and made legitimate allowance for whatever was unusual in the week, I couldn't help but smile at the crass idiocy of these 'men of the world' who are so sure that parsons are out of touch with life. It states but the barest fact to say that many a minister sees more of 'life' in a month than some of his critics see in five years. The very privacy of the matters with which he deals forbids plain mention of them, but for others ignorantly to conclude that pastoral work is drinking interminable cups of tea, and engaging in hours of small talk, is an error so grotesque that it demands contradiction.

People say sometimes that the minister sees people at their best, the lawyer sees them at their worst, and the doctor sees them as they are. We *do* see people at their best!—but their best moments are often moments of confession when they must needs reveal themselves at their worst. After twenty years of hearing the voluntary confessions of people, there is little new to hear. All the sex perversions have been poured over you: you know the mind now of harlots who have been vending their bodies for years and were unshakably sure (till Christ called them) that all men are hunters: you will have gone round—as I have done more than once—with the converted burglar returning the 'swag': you will have heard fifty times of the 'double life' of people you had supposed were happily wed. Some men will still imagine that you know nothing of life. Not noticing your presence, a man will pour out a spate of filthy language and apologize to you for his disregard of the cloth. He may

F

even hint that he is sure you have never heard language like that before. If he only knew! In my Army days I classified all bad language into three categories: cussing, obscenities, and blasphemy. Obscenity and blasphemy I could never endure. Cussing I came hardly to notice. One must talk to someone!

All this experience of life lies behind preaching—experience in the ministry and experience before one entered the ministry. These darker themes are not the normal staple of preaching but familiarity with them gives a penetrating insight into the human heart! Baffled souls feel understood. The man who comes to worship only occasionally (and perhaps to sneer) knows when preaching is close to life: may even have his own evil past read for him: finds a vigour in his conscience he has not known in years. . . .

It can be said, without fear of intelligent contradiction, that powerful preaching requires an intimate knowledge of the human heart, and it is in his privileged office as pastor, as well as in his own pursuit of goodness, that the preacher gathers his unusual knowledge of men.

There are, of course, still men who 'fancy' themselves as preachers and despise the pastoral office. There is an oft-told story of Dr. W. L. Watkinson, the distinguished preacher, that he was once approached by the officers of his church with a request that he would kindly undertake a little more pastoral visitation. According to the story, he is said to have put his feet on his desk, and said to the deputation: 'You can either have my head or my feet. I will visit you, or preach to you. I can't do both.'

It is a ridiculous story, which I always hope has no basis in truth, but, if it has, it reflects upon the reputation of that distinguished man. The story draws a false distinction between the office of pastor and preacher: it

mistakenly assumes that a man can preach close to his
people's need who never shepherds them: it falsely
implies that a consecrated man hasn't time for doing
both. When we recall that so great a preacher as
Alexander Whyte shepherded his flock with loving care:
when we remember how George Morrison of Wellington, with a membership in his church of over 1,800
people, 'covered the ground': when we think on the
loving pastoral heart of Watts-Ditchfield, the first Bishop
of Chelmsford, we lesser men have no excuse for offering
our people a choice between our head and our feet.

I want us to look at that distinction a little more
closely: I mean, the distinction of pastor and preacher.
It is true, of course, that the offices of pastor and preacher
are distinguishable in thought, and different in emphasis.
We often say that to be a good preacher one must be a
good speaker, and to be a good pastor one must be a
good listener; but it is far, far nearer to the heart of this
question to insist that the offices are closely inter-related,
and that no man can hope to be a fully effective preacher
who fails to be a shepherd of his flock.

In the first place, unless he is in close and intimate
touch with his people, he cannot know what to preach
about. Speaking broadly, his task on Sunday is to
answer, with all the richness of theological and biblical
scholarship that he can command, the questions his
people have been asking him—perhaps unconsciously—
in the week. That, I suppose, is why John Kelman said:
'I cannot *preach* under a thousand visits a year.' Nothing
keeps preaching closer to reality than for the preacher to
keep close to the people themselves. Moreover, the
preacher has no way of judging the true effectiveness of
his preaching unless the same intimacy holds. How can
he tell whether the series of sermons on the difficulties of

prayer really cleared the difficulties up? How can he discover whether his counsel concerning the conquest of this particular sin or that had practical worth, unless he is among the people to find out?

When I was a student, and much admiring (as I do still) the rich and painstaking service of my tutors, I used to think that the highest exercise of the ministerial office was to be a tutor, too. Other students have entertained the same idea. Robertson Nicoll said, when he was at college, he held that opinion also, and that it was commonly shared by the keener students of his time. Afterwards, he changed his mind. To have a cure of souls, he came to believe, is the highest task to which any minister can be called. To stand in the pulpit on a Sunday and see the eager and expectant faces of the people turned towards you, and know they have come for worship and for the bit of bread that you have been preparing for them in the week; to feel, as you look at them: 'These are my people'; to know that in all the great hours of their life, when they want to be wed, when a child is born into their home, when trouble comes, when the doctor is going in and out, when bereavement robs them of every scrap of joy—to know that in that hour the door is open, and you not only may go but you must go; that the cry of their heart then is for their minister . . . to dwell upon that is to know a joy which, to my mind, not even the unquestioned delights of scholarly research can surpass. To receive the confidence of people; to know the secrets they have told to no other living soul; to blush with them over their sins and exult with them when the sin is flung under the table; to know their private affairs and to be the sharer of their highest ideals, is to have a joy of which not one of us is really worthy. How to make ourselves the more effective in it is the task to which we must turn our attention now, and to observe, as its glorious by-product, how splendidly it serves the pulpit all the time.

II

If we are to live in our people's lives and know them individually, the question arises: 'How can this best be done?' Shall we meet them in *their* homes, in *our* home, or in our vestry? Each of these places has some advantage over the others. Let us glance at each of them in turn.

To call on them in their homes is the normal method of pastoral visitation. It is the necessary way with the people who will not come to us, and with the sick. It is great to get into our people's homes: to see the circumstances in which they live: to get a picture of their background: to carry the spirit of the Church to their hearthside and receive their confidences beneath their own roof. This kind of pastoral work must always be done. There is no method of shepherding the people which will entirely eliminate the labour of going from door to door.

Some men give an afternoon a week to knocking on the doors of people they *don't* know in an effort to reach the people who are outside the Church. Or they pay special attention to the parents of any children in their Sunday School or Youth Activities who have, as yet, no other link with the Church. Or, when they call on a Church member, they enquire if anyone in the immediate neighbourhood has, or has had in time past, the frailest link with the Church, and they call with that as a point of contact and try to strengthen the connection.

Yet door to door visitation has its disadvantages so far as Church members are concerned. The people may be out—though it is still of some advantage that they find your card when they return. Or it may be impossible to get the conversation beyond the most utter trivialities, which is understandable, of course, in the early stages, and with nervous people, but which seems a dreadful waste of hours if it happens half-a-dozen times on one afternoon; or other people may be present, and anything like intimate conversation be debarred.

Consequently, some men use their own home as a second way of getting to know their people. They let it be understood in the church that on one night in the week they will always be in—and in for their people to call. I met a man recently who had made that his rule for years and had rigidly kept it up. He told me that in the last four years he had never been left without callers on a single night. The friendliness of one's home encourages confidences. In the intimacy of the fireside, folk often talk from their heart, and understanding can be established out of which still deeper confidences can come.

Yet even this method has its faults. Confidences of the deeper kind are only possible one with one, and this you cannot guarantee. It is seldom that you have just one person present. Many friends slip in, and, as the happy conversation widens, it often loses depth and necessarily becomes less personal. Good has been done. The family of the church is knit together in hours like these and old barriers are broken down, but the best and most persistent use of this method will convince you, I think, that some other approach is *still* needed. This, I believe, you will discover, as I have discovered myself, is to be found in the regular use of your vestry for pastoral work.

Fix on a certain day and, if possible, certain hours, and let it be known that you are there to deal with people one by one in their spiritual need. You are not there to talk with a woman who just wants to gossip. You are not there for those who have half-an-hour to waste, and would like to waste it with you. You are there specifically to help people in their personal problems, and, as the months go by, your purpose will be understood. Here you have privacy. Here you are secure from the door-bell and the telephone. Here people can open their heart to you with the freedom and unhurriedness which are essential for the private things they have to tell. If, at first, you give a general invitation to people to come, you may have the experience of finding, as I found in early days, that many more people came than you could cope with on one evening, and you may have the sad experience of needing to go over to the waiting-room and tell them that it will not be possible for you to see them all that night. This will drive you, quite naturally, to the use of an appointments book, and you will divide the time up into, say, half-hour periods to begin with, and people can come at a precise time, and know how long they will have to stay. To deny that the work is very costly to heart and mind would be idle, but, at the end of nearly every such day, you will take your tired way home with a light heart and you will feel deeply within yourself that, in hours like these, you are, indeed, a minister of God: that awful sense of irrelevance in the community, and utter ineffectiveness in the work which seems to haunt some men, will leave you. Whoever else gets afflicted with the fashionable 'inferiority complex', it will not be you. Humble in heart, you will, of course, give the glory to God, but the joy of being His dependable servant will break over you again and again.

When I have commended this method of pastoral work to some of my ministerial friends, they have objected to it on the ground that the people would not come. Some of them say that they have tried the method and proved what they anticipated: the people did not come. I cannot feel that this is a fatal objection. I have come to believe that there is some kind of problem in nearly everybody's life, and there are always some people who have reached the hour when they must speak of the perplexities that are on their mind. It may, indeed, be necessary to entice people to come at first and, until it becomes a settled and natural thing in the church, some little element of constraint may be necessary for them. But if they feel that you are a man who has something to give away, and are yearning over them all the time, they will not long resist you. Have your appointments book ready. When somebody comments at the end of the service on the helpfulness, or, it may be, the unhelpfulness, of the sermon, suggest to him that he comes and talks the thing over with you in your vestry. Be precise in the matter of time. Tell him that you will expect him, and you are sure that, in personal conversation, you could help one another. Slowly, it will become a normal part of the church's life, and for the people to seek an interview of this character with the minister will be as normal as saying their prayers.

III

What are the chief problems that the people bring when they come in this way? On what topics ought we be especially equipped to speak? If I may draw freely on my own experience, I should suggest these as the topics on which people most freely come and talk.

(1) There are *the people to whom God is not real:* who are seeking a spiritual experience: who have been provoked, perhaps, by a sermon to say that God is not real to them, and that He never has been, and that it is not

their fault. No pastor of souls can ask a better opportunity to commend his Lord than that. When the time
comes for meeting them, draw them out in conversation;
ask them about their spiritual pilgrimage and what, in
religion, they *are* sure about, and then seek the barrier in
them to that fuller revelation that God is willing to give.
Quite often they are amazingly ignorant themselves as
to the things which hinder God going further with them.
There may be some deep resentment in their life, some
unsurrendered sin, some habit which is spiritually debilitating but the danger of which they do not fully understand. To make a little progress with them at the first
talk, and then go further a week later, is, perhaps, as
much as can be hoped, but, step by step, you will lead
them on until the day comes when you meet for no
other purpose than to go with them into the church that,
kneeling at the Communion Rail, they may consecrate
their lives anew to God. I need hardly say that this work
is most costly in time. It cannot very well be otherwise.
Souls are not adequately dealt with by a swift ten
minutes in an 'inquiry room', and a pastor must be
prodigal with time if he is going to shepherd his people
into all the richness of the faith.

(2) Many people come with *problems of* their *prayer*
life. I think it will amaze you when you get to know
your people well to discover how little some of them
pray, and how perfunctory are the prayers of others. It
will surprise you too, I think, to know what crude ideas
some of them have about the theory of prayer, and what
bitterness there is in the heart of others because the
prayers they have offered seem to have received no reply.
If worship and prayer are at the very heart of the devotional life, as most of us believe, how important it is that
we should be masters of the devotional life ourselves,

and equipped to instruct our people in how to speak with God. All that one can learn from the saints and from one's own experience will be requisitioned by the people who come needing to be taught to pray.

(3) Other people come with *intellectual problems*. I know that many people who come with intellectual problems are really, consciously or unconsciously, concealing beneath the intellectual problem, a moral problem too. It is important, however, that we do not assume too readily that this is the case. There are genuine intellectual difficulties in the mind of our people which are not related to moral failure at all, and, while it is important to bear that possibility in mind, it would be a grievous, and I nearly said a vulgar, mistake to assume in every case that they are concealing something on the moral plane. One of the finest lay preachers I have ever known —an honours graduate, and a high-school master—came to me first with certain theories concerning Spinoza and his doctrine of Theism. I never felt as grateful before, or since, that I had read Spinoza with some closeness, but if we began with Spinoza, we ended at the Cross. If there were moral problems in that man's life—and there were—the intellectual problems were real also, and a careless and unsympathetic treatment of them would have put him off. All we have gathered of solid learning, every scrap of apologetics that we know, and all the fruits of our own hard thinking concerning the problems of providence, will be of use.

Nor need we forget the social problems. Many young people are sincerely held by Communism. Some of them have keen minds. They believe they have found in Communism the answer to the problems of race and class, and they pursue their ideal with a passion and readiness of sacrifice which might well shame some

Christians. 'The trouble with you Christians is that you do not know the meaning of sacrificial love', said one of them the other day. 'I always believed that only the power of Christ could change men's lives, but now I have seen them changed by Communism.' If the vestry door is open, and it is known that you are available, you are, at least, giving an opportunity of conversation to the lad tempted to exchange Jesus for Karl Marx.

(4) One of the most difficult set of problems which will be brought to your attention will be that which centres in *domestic incompatibility*. People (some of them in the Church, and others who belong to no Church at all) come to you for advice concerning the unhappiness and maladjustment of their home. In my opinion, no cases are more unfruitful than these, unless you can get one, or both, of them (as you will constantly endeavour) into a real relationship with Christ. Unless they are ready for a full and deep surrender to God, the old trouble is patched up and breaks out again later—as much of the work of Marriage Guidance Clinics goes to confirm. I have come to the conclusion that to take the higher and harder line and seek to bring them to the Cross and constrain them to take Our Lord's attitude to the situation, is to do a bit of work which really *does* deal with the thing in its depth, and is the only possible way by which an effective cure will be found.

(5) *Nerve cases* are another common group. If any man lets it be known that he has some understanding and skill at helping people in nervous disorder, there is a shuffle of feet on his doorstep at once. Some of the suppliants only want health. They may even come in asking you whether they are speaking to a minister or a 'psychologist', because they do not want religion. Yet many people who come seeking a physician of the mind

can be led to discover, also, a Saviour of their soul.

It may seem from this that no man can undertake the work unless he has some expert knowledge of psychology, but I am convinced myself that, even with a modest knowledge of psychology, you can do the most urgent task that is required. You may not be able to resolve a neurosis, but it will be no small achievement if you can recognize it. If you are in a city of any size, you will know the people who are practising psycho-therapy, and who are practising it in a Christian way. For the expert help you are not able to give you can direct the seekers to those who *are* able to give it, and in the aspects of the trouble which are spiritual you can still stand by and see them through.

(6) Another general group of people who seek personal conversation with the minister are those who have *a truant heart towards the Church*. Perhaps they are thinking of leaving the fellowship, possibly because of some personal difference with another member, or because they have been attracted to some other Body of Believers. In a large church there are often people who feel drawn, perhaps, to the music or ritual of those Churches which use elaborate ceremonial, or, on the other hand, by the simplicities of the Quaker Meeting, and who have come to feel that the Church of their fathers does not meet their need. In many cases, they just drift away. Afterwards, they are heard to complain, it may be unjustly, that nobody detained them. But they cannot say that in a church where everybody knows that the minister is laying himself out in order to be of use to his people: that the door of his vestry stands open for anyone with a serious concern on his, or her, mind, and that each of these problems would be talked out with patient understanding. The fact must be faced that some souls will

find richer pasture in a Communion other than the one in which they grew up, but they ought to be quite sure of that before they go. Even then they should pause. A man owes a debt to his Church, as to his home and his country, and in any hour when loyalty is challenged, he ought not to dwell chiefly on 'What can I get?' but also on 'What do I owe?' and 'What can I give?' Yet people inwardly troubled like this ought to meet such sympathetic understanding at this time of unrest that, even if they finally seek a spiritual abode elsewhere, they will retain the tenderest recollections of their early spiritual home.

(7) *Sex problems* bring many people to the vestry door. Anybody who does this personal pastoral work will admit that the sex problem is ever before us, and in many varied forms: youths in the grip of masturbation: young people who have been convinced of the needlessness of respecting moral prohibitions when they are engaged to be wed: people fighting a constant, and, oftentimes, a losing battle with impure thoughts: homosexuals: and the sodomites and catamites. . . . If Christ has—as we believe—'a sovereign balm for every wound', it would be honest to admit that we seem not always able to apply it to these needy souls. Some, it is true, find a full release, and others claim and receive the power they need to endure. If we cannot unpick the nature of those born awry, we can give them a comradeship of understanding they have not found elsewhere, and often guide them into sublimated service and peace of heart.

(8) Finally, there are those who come, as we have said, just to *confess*. They do not normally open the conversation with that word but they cannot conceal their burdened conscience. If the Roman Church is wrong in

insisting upon frequent confession by everybody, and always to the priest, the Protestant Churches have been wrong in making no provision for it at all. There are times when even the most robust Protestant feels a longing for someone strangely like a confessor. Indeed, those Protestant ministers who have that mystic gift of drawing confidences say that the difference between them and the Roman Catholic priests is not only that in the Roman Catholic Church the confessions are compelled but that the Roman priest can fix the hour when he will receive confessions, and they receive them unbidden at all hours of the day!

There is, of course, something to learn in hearing the confession of sins. One's love and sympathy invite it and make it possible, but it is not well to press hard for confidences beyond the point at which they are freely given. It needs not to be said with what utter secrecy we guard all we hear (and that means secrecy from your wife also), nor check the sad recital by looking shocked at what they tell. All the stored wisdom of life we need in giving counsel—especially where restitution is possible, and the sin of others also is involved but must not be betrayed. To point the penitents to the Saviour at the last and convince them that 'He delighteth in mercy' . . . 'O what a happiness is this!'

This, then, is to indicate some of the problems on which people are seeking help, and the kind of equipment we ought to possess for their service. It is so costly in time and strength that no one can sustain the demand except as God gives him an aching love for the people. The secret of the pastoral office is in the word 'caring'. This loving care cannot be faked. A large departmental store sent an apologetic letter to a customer the other day, but the letter came to grief in the typewriter. It included this sentence: 'Although hundreds of letters and telephone calls come to us each day, we fake a personal interest in each one.' The minister who fakes a personal interest in each of his members will not deceive them for long. The man who truly loves them will leave each one of them feeling that, in point of fact, he has a particular concern over them and there is a special bond. Dean Briggs of Harvard had this gift. If you ask an old Harvard man if he knew Briggs, the chances are that he will answer: 'Did I know him? I knew him as perhaps nobody else knew him. There was a special bond between us.' He is unaware that all the other men are saying the same thing. Briggs didn't fake the affection. He cared for his men like that, but so rich was his humanity that every one who drew on it felt that he was having it all. It is like that with a devoted pastor. Anybody in need feels that he has all of him. Indeed, the saints have even said so much about God. 'God was giving His whole mind to my case as though He had no other soul in the universe to save and sanctify but me.'

Young men might well feel unequal to the pastorate as they survey all the difficult subjects on which people may turn to them for help. But they need not be overwhelmed. Some of these problems are not often brought to *young* men, and every year lived close to God and to the people will help in equipping one to deal with the questions when they come.

Sometimes ministers—no longer young—feel that they are failures at this work. They seem to lack that mystic gift of drawing confidences. People just do *not* turn to them. They wonder if it is their misfortune or their fault.

Only God can make this clear to a man—though He might use as His agent the minister's frank, affectionate friend. But here are some questions a man might take into the quietness of an honest self-examination—even though no frank, affectionate friend should be at hand.

Do I really *love* the people?

Have I *time* for them—and make them know it?

Or do I secretly feel that half the things they want to talk to me about are trifles beneath my notice?

Have I come to love books more than men and women? Has learning turned into 'academics' with me, and am I pursuing scholarship for itself and not as the servant of my pulpit and my people?

Do I wish myself out of the pastorate, and into some other situation where I have not the care of souls? Am I—so far as this congregation is concerned—a hireling and not a shepherd?

And if I am guilty on any, or all, of these counts, where can I find the answer? Can a man find it on his knees? Is there a supernatural love given by God to the shepherds of the flock, and if I ask Him will He give me 'a passion for souls'?

Ask, and it shall be given you; seek, and ye shall find; knock, and it shall be opened unto you.

SIX

THE PERILS OF THE CALLING

DOCTORS of medicine classify certain ailments as
'occupational diseases'. Men are in danger of getting
them because they follow a certain calling. The miner
is prone to pneumoconiosis and nystagmus. The quarry-
man is subject to silicosis, and lead painters to lead colic.
Surprising as some people would find it, the ministry is
subject to occupational diseases as well. Not all men
are attacked, and, perhaps, not many succumb, but it is
important that we know where the dangers lie and be
on our guard against them.

I

Some of these dangers are not peculiar to our calling.
They are grounded in the human nature we share with
other sinners, but they may come upon us with peculiar
force by reason of the work we do and the circumstances
in which we do it.

1. *Women* have been a source of temptation to men
since time began. Some men feel the temptation more
powerfully than others. Blessed by an even temperament, disciplined in virtue from his youth up, happily
wed, and strict in his devotions, a man may barely feel a
tremor of the passions which shake another man to his
soul. Yet, the least tested of men would be foolish to
suppose that he is beyond temptation here. A sudden
change in circumstances might put him in the fire.

G

Widowers have their own battles to fight. Age alone grants no exemptions. Temptations to the sins of the flesh are never very far away.

In Chile, before 1932, people would point to Mount Descabezado and explain that it was once a terrible volcano. Long ago! Before dependable history! But for centuries it had been extinct.

Then came that awful day in April 1932, when Descabezado blew its top off, and covered vast areas of Chile and the Argentine with an awful pall of smoke, and blotted the sun from the heavens for towns that were fifty miles away.

Let no man say, concerning the sins of the flesh, that they have entirely gone because he is no longer young. David thought that. Noah too. And many a man in modern life. We are especially prone to temptation when we have a proud and settled conviction that it cannot come.

If the minister of God is specially fortified in some ways against the sins of the flesh, he is, in others, especially vulnerable. People often confess to God through him. Women do. They have, on occasion, sad stories to tell. Most of them are broken penitents, and it is a clean, clear task to lift them up and point them to the Saviour. But now and then one finds an evil woman in the guise of a penitent. She confesses almost with relish. She is lascivious even at the mercy seat. She can burn with desire in the presence of a man of God.

God does not leave His servant unwarned in that hour. All the hosts of heaven stand guard about those who are keeping close to Him. But, perhaps, only one other calling is more dangerous in this way, and there is complete safety only on one's knees.

2. *Money*—or, rather, the lack of it—is another

common source of peril. Ministers share these difficulties, of course, with laymen, but again their calling adds its own peculiarity of circumstance.

A minister is poor, but he cannot *look* poor. The honour of God and the Church is involved to some extent in his appearance. Folk can contemptuously dismiss this talk of 'keeping up appearances' as being vanity, but there is more in it than that. Both the Church and the neighbourhood feel the unfitness of things when the minister of God is shabby and ill-groomed.

Moreover, the minister goes frequently into homes better furnished than his own. Even the natural and proper desire to give pleasure to his wife might seduce him from that firm frugality by which alone he can honourably live. Washing-machines, refrigerators, and television sets can be very appealing. Some ministerial situations almost—though not quite—demand a car. With the cost of living soaring, and income lagging seriously behind, it is so easy to get into debt and so hard to get out of it.

More cases of ministerial discipline arise over these problems than any other. The work of God in a country town can be damaged for years by a man who moves on and leaves a legacy of debts. He will have to preach many good sermons to make up for the harm he has done to the cause of God. For men without private means, and wives without private means, only the strictest economy enables one to get through, and every personal indulgence—especially heavy smoking—must be watched with the vigilance that it demands.

3. *Laziness* is a sin which can tempt laymen and ministers alike, but, again, the ministerial calling puts the peril in its own peculiar way.

As we have already noticed, ministers are largely the

masters of their own time. Many a lazy layman—however hard he finds it—must keep his hours in mine or mill, or he will be dismissed. Millions of the workers of the world begin their day's toil by feeding a card into a clock which records with cold precision their moment of arrival. No clock records the minister's hour of beginning, and no machine can measure the earnestness with which he goes at his work once he has begun. If a man's conscience concerning time gets dulled through the years, it is amazing how busy he can *feel* while he is doing very little.

Because—here is the subtlety of it—a man can be lazy at ministerial work without going too frequently to the golf links or to some other form of recreation. He can delude himself that he is 'studying' when he is idling the working hours away with some gossip's reminiscences, instead of wrestling with a deep theological work. He can suppose he is 'hard at it' when whole mornings are swallowed up on business trifles best left to the odd half-hours of his day, and he can even suppose that a 'set' of sermons made years ago will do, in a slightly re-hashed form, for the congregation he is facing now.

When his ministerial brethren remarked to Dr. J. H. Jowett at a fraternal that their studies were constantly interrupted by the telephone, Jowett was perplexed. He could only say that *his* studies were not interrupted that way.

But then he began his working day all his life at 6 a.m. People are not bothering you on the telephone at 6 a.m. Nor—so I have found, who work best late at night—do they ring you at midnight. The silent hours speed past in solid work.

We shall find the answer to this peril—as to so many others—in a disciplined devotional life. A man who goes over his day each evening with God will not long remain satisfied with pottering, sluggishness, and days half frittered away.

II

I turn next to those perils which are not by any means unknown outside our holy calling but which come nearer, perhaps, to being our 'occupational diseases' than those I have mentioned already.

1. The itch for *popularity* can be a real peril to a preacher. He wants the crowd. Of course! He has something to say of immense importance.

O that the world *might taste and see* . . .

And there is nothing wrong in the desire at that stage. Indeed, if a young preacher were to say that he had no desire for the crowd, one would wonder, first, at his sincerity, and, then, at his confidence in the message he had to give.

George Savile said: 'Popularity is a crime from the moment it is sought: it is a virtue when men have it whether they will or no.' Savile was thinking of politics rather than preaching and I cannot go with him in his second clause. Popularity isn't a virtue: it is an opportunity. The peril for the preacher arises in his temptation to seek popularity by unworthy means, or hold it by the same soiled device.

It seeks to seduce him in these ways. It may lead him away from the simplicity and reproach of the Gospel. He may become more concerned to say something new than something true. He may 'stunt', clutching at any modern interest or craze, and talking of the events of the passing hour rather than of 'the faith once delivered to the saints'. He aims to be smart rather than deep:

brilliant rather than discerning: clever rather than helpful: interesting more than disturbing.

People soon tire of it. If such an occupation were not, in itself, a betrayal of his trust, it would still be incapable of doing what he wishes. Crowds caught in that way are not held.

No man, I imagine, was ever made especially happy in the eventide of his life by the simple recollection that the crowds had gathered to hear him preach. 'What did I do with the crowd?' would be, I imagine, the question much on his mind. 'Did I lend myself so completely to the Holy Spirit that He convicted them of sin, exalted the Saviour, and called those sinners home?' If he had not an easy conscience in the face of questions like that, nothing else could comfort him.

Yet the itch for popularity is not only a peril to the minister in his preaching. It can be a peril in his private life as well.

Some ministers feel foolishly cut off by their office from other men. They do not humbly accept that subtle degree of separation which their ordination involves. They are so eager to be regarded as 'a man among men' that they seize opportunities of doing the unministerial thing in a pathetic effort to win popularity. The chaplain will sometimes tipple in the mess. The factory padre tells a risqué story in the canteen. The parson will give advice on the pools' permutations.

And all these efforts are as futile as they are pathetic. What people want in their heart of hearts of a minister of God, is that he be a minister of God. Just that! Anything that soils the image in their hearts is a sad and staining thing, and most sad and most staining when it comes from the minister himself.

Do not scorn popularity. Take it, if it comes, as a

trust from God. Marvel—as you well may—that you have it and better men have not. And employ all your wits to use it for the greater glory of God.

2. I almost shrink from mentioning the next thing in my mind. It is *jealousy*. Perhaps it would shock the laity if they knew we had this to face. They expect ballet dancers, and chorus girls, and music-hall comediennes, and film stars to be jealous of one another . . . but ministers of God! Is it possible?

Alas! It is not only possible: it is actual. We know it by observing others, and we know it by observing ourselves. *Lord, have mercy upon us!*

It arises often from the popularity we mentioned just now: the popularity of someone else. Not always, or often, in our conscious mind, but at some level of our mental life, we seem to pose the question to ourselves: 'What has he got that I haven't got?' and we are not always honest with the answer. We do not willingly admit the possession in others of gifts denied to us. We cannot sincerely sing

> *The gift which He on one bestows,*
> *We all delight to prove.*

The fruit of their hard work we deny as readily as their gifts, and we suppose the people to be fooled who run after them. Even when we cannot avoid praising them, because others are doing so, we do it grudgingly and with a flavour of disparagement.

'Yes! He *does* hold the people, doesn't he? It is just that little touch of humour, you know. . . .'

'His grip on folk through the years is *quite* astonishing. Of course, he appeals to women most. . . .'

'I couldn't call him deep. It's those little stories he tells. The ordinary people like them. . . .'

Just a nuance. But no discerning person misses it—or misses the cause of it. This is the devil doing his damnedest in what may be a fine mind. And how he throws the fuel on the fire. 'He hasn't a mind like yours. . . . He doesn't carry your weight of scholarship. . . . What has he written that matters? O yes! but it is all light stuff. . . .'

No man is really free until he is free of this. And this kind cometh not out save by prayer. So—once again—*Lord, have mercy upon us.*

3. There is a danger of *professionalism*, I suppose, in all professions, but it always seems especially heinous in the ministry.

If a lawyer is accurate, no one will accuse him for not having his heart in conveyancing, but if a minister buries the dead without feeling, and marries the young lovers as though by rote, something precious is missing and people are aware of it.

What has happened to a man guilty of professionalism?

He is almost certainly neglecting his private devotions, and he has ceased to believe in a high way himself of the things he is called to do. Familiarity with holy things has made him slightly contemptuous of them. In pastoral visitation, he does not feel himself a visitor of God to men and women. He does it because 'the people expect it'. In preaching, he does not come as from the audience chamber of Heaven, hot with a message from the Almighty, but he says something at the appointed time because . . . well, it *is* the appointed time. He touches the eternities—birth and death—with the same mechanical motions and, because it means so little to him, it comes to mean little to the people.

It will be said, in defence of men guilty of failure here, that no one can perform these offices week after week for years, and feel any awe about them. But that is plainly not true. Thousands of devout ministers retain a freshness in their work decade after decade. Their reverent happiness at the wedding is barely exceeded by that of the bridegroom: their joy as they talk to the young parents on the baptism of their first babe reveals their own delighted wonder at this new gift of God: their conduct of the solemn service of burial makes it clear that they are mourning with those that mourn. . . .

The sovereign way to avoid all of these perils is in a life of intimate communion with God.

4. Allied with the danger of professionalism is that of *intellectual snobbery*.

Educated laymen might wonder today on what we base our superiorities, and that there is a large admixture of vanity in this sin it would be impossible to deny.

But it arises, I think, in this way. A minister of religion—especially in a rural area—can have a somewhat lonely life. His interests, maybe, are mostly academic. Even though he may visit his people with regularity, he may find conversation difficult the moment it gets beyond the crops, and the cow which recently calved. It may not be his good fortune—as it is the good fortune of some men in rural areas—to have in his flock folk who read wide and think hard, and bit by bit he may find himself living largely alone in a world of his own.

As a pastor of God he should still cherish his flock, and make people his hobby, but more and more his life is lived in books, and less and less with men and women. A sense of superiority grows in his soul. He judges folk, not in the wholeness of their personality, but by their *knowledge*, and here his people seem small. He does not heed enough their courage. He does not see the greatness which stands up so bravely to the disasters of life,

H

nor realize that almost every man knows something he does not know himself. His latent sense of superiority infects his manner, and in all his dealings with the people he appears to be upon a platform. He talks down to people and (not unnaturally) they resent it.

Years ago, I was shown, in the municipal offices of the town where I lived, a letter from a local cleric who had written to put them right on some matter of public concern. I have seldom read anything more compounded of academic superiority and business ignorance, but I could not enjoy the roars of laughter in the municipal office. The learned fool was utterly out of touch with life, and utterly unaware of it. It gave me to understand a little more of the amused scorn in which some laymen regard the cloth.

5. *Self-pity* is not a peril only of the ministry but, again, we meet it in a special form. Our occupation is, in some ways, nervously exhausting. There is a spiritual expenditure which has physical consequences. Keeping close to his work, and knowing nothing, perhaps, of relaxation and recuperation, a man may soon find himself spent.

The experience often follows a time of spiritual exaltation. A reaction sets in. Young men, unused to these rhythmic laws, and uninstructed as yet in how to deal with themselves in such an hour, may feel overwhelmed and lapse into moodiness. Little as some laymen would be willing to concede it, ours is a hard vocation. A man may believe himself unwanted. 'What real difference in the community would it make if I gave up altogether?' he may ask himself. Or he may feel at times over-preached. The pulpit and people seem to demand more than he has to give. If the field he is ploughing is hard, and the measurable results negligible, it isn't surprising if the spirit flags a little, and depression assails him. Increasing his own effort, as an earnest man will do at such a time, he may cut out his recreation altogether, and fall physically below par, and then self-pity, that spiritually debilitating disease, walks in.

What is the answer to self-pity?

Let a man plainly recognize the fact if the body is not having its due. Let him aim to get a walk each day and learn also how to relax. Let him rest his mind from spiritual problems in the love and wisdom and beauty and peace of God. Let him recognize that self-pity is such a *cowardly* thing. Whatever else it is, and however provoking circumstances are, self-pity isn't brave. Let him think on the courage with which people in his flock are bearing the major distresses of life: how they are standing up to their bereavements, and grave sicknesses, and deep distresses, with faith and fortitude, and let him ask himself if their shepherd can be less brave than they. And, most of all, let him learn that he is not living on his own reserves but on the limitless resources of God, and he will direct his pity where it belongs—not inwards to his own undoing, but outwards to the needy souls who are all around.

6. It may seem strange if I say that the ministry is in peril of *pettiness*, but I do not know how more accurately to describe the state of mind that I mean.

It happens sometimes that a church includes a little group of malcontents who keep up a continual barrage of grumbling. They drip adverse words about everything which is going on. Their attitude is one of settled opposition. They impute in subtle ways, perhaps, that the minister is not completely dedicated, or not sound in the faith, or not as zealous as his predecessor, or not quite the man 'this church needs'.

Not only are these people an irritant in the life of the church: they can rob the minister of his peace and poise, and even trap him into pettiness. He may find himself in a state of inner irritation whenever they appear, and he may be tricked by their nattering into foolish judgements, hasty words, and even sharp retaliation. Their conduct dictates his own. Instead of meeting their smallness with largeness, he becomes similarly petty, constantly on edge, disturbed even in his prayer life, and sometimes the leader of a faction rather than the minister of the whole church.

How can a man be on his guard against this?

Let him do what St. Augustine advised. Let him take the statements of his critics and ask God to confirm or contradict what they say. There *may* be something in their criticisms. If there is only a little, why not learn it? Turn your opponents into your servants. The rest? —throw it away.

But go further. Ask yourself: 'Why is this man such a troubler? What is gnawing him inside? This is clearly the expression of some past experience, or present dislike; some fear, worry, sin. . . . In any case it is spiritual need, and I am the spiritual doctor. What can I do about it? How can I even get him to consult me for his own ailment? . . .'

When a minister is thinking at that point, he has found the answer to this peril because, if he is not yet an expert doctor of souls, he is certainly not petty.

7. *Repenting our sacrifices* is the only way I can describe the next peril I have in mind.

Not all men, but many men, make a sacrifice when they answer God's call to the ministry. The same quality of life: the same mental acumen, and the same persistence in study which has led to their acceptance for the ministry would almost certainly have won for them a ready entrance into some other profession—and a profession better paid.

To a young man, tingling with a sense of call, all that is as nothing. He is proud to make the sacrifice. He is not thinking what he has given up but only what he has gained.

But the years roll by. The vision dims a little. One feels the difficulties of the work. People are not as eager for the Word as one hoped. Awkward people—as we have just admitted—have to be handled, and the lean frugality of the ministerial life must be borne. One must look at a shilling, not twice, but several times. The hardness of the life, in some ways, comes home, and there is no prospect that it will improve. The easier times to which the rising young business man looks forward are not normally for the minister of God.

Meanwhile, one's contemporaries at school are forging ahead in their chosen professions. Many of them are doing well. They wave to us from their new cars. Their wives are better clad than ours. Their children have things our children must go without. Their continental holidays make our break seem like a day's excursion. . . . Sometimes something stirs in our heart. Is it envy? God forgive us!—it *seems* like envy. Maybe, we should not have felt like this if we had been obviously successful in the ministry, but our sacrifice seems of no avail even to God. We are toying with the thought that *we* might have been where those laymen are! If it required brains and application, and if school was anything to go by, well, we could have given old John a lead. We are repenting our sacrifices: half wishing we had not taken this road: juggling with the idea that we could still have served God as a layman but had a spoon in the flesh-pots of Egypt as well. . . .

O God! Is this the man who told the fathers of the Church that he was called to preach: that Christ Himself had broken the silence of eternity, spoken his name, and handed him a commission from His pierced hand: that he was ready to leave all things and follow his Lord . . .?

A minister is seldom so low as when, like Lot's wife, he repents his sacrifice, and looks back.

8. There is a special sense in which a minister can be guilty of *failing his children*.

All men must relax sometimes, mentally as well as physically. If a man is always consciously 'on guard'; if he can never open his heart freely; if he cannot occasionally 'explode', life will become a great strain for that man. It is true that, as he grows in grace, serenity will more and more possess his soul, and even the desire to 'explode' will come rarely, but he will still need to open his heart, and home is the natural place to do it.

A wise and silent wife is, of course, the best confidante. He can pour out his heart to her, and benefit by her counsel at the same time as he knows that her lips are guarded on all the things he tells. And even to his own wife he never imparts other people's secrets without their permission. It is in his *own* perplexities that her understanding sympathy can be so valuable, and her independent judgement so useful as well.

But the peril a minister with a family is always in concerns the children. He may 'explode' in front of them. He may speak with asperity about some woman gossip in the church, or with jealousy of a colleague, or with scorn of some malcontent in the fellowship, and, unaware of it himself, he is damaging his own children. He damages them whether his asperity and scorn are justified or not. If it is unjustified, the child will come to think that father (though a minister of God) is no different from other men, and, if it is justified, the child may suppose that churches are made up of nasty or awkward people, and get a loathing rather than a love for the family of God. If the minister succumbs to some of these other perils we have pointed out—laziness, self-pity, pettiness—from whomsoever else he may conceal them, he will not conceal them from his children. The ones who, in his best moments, he most wants to win, will be those who, by his own undisciplined life, he has impeded on their way to the Kingdom.

Yet—lest any man lash himself more than he ought—we do well to remember that we cannot compel our children into the Kingdom. Some who have lived near their Lord, and wrapped their children in prayer from the month of their conception, have not had the crowning happiness of seeing their children pressing on in this way of life. But they pray on.

9. We come now to the peril which is chief of all perils: *neglecting our devotions*. If a man will win here, he can win everywhere. He need, indeed, do no more than glance at the formidable list of perils we have set out in order to recognize the direction from which the danger might come. Then he can toss them all aside. Guarded devotions secure success all along the line. Vigilance here means victory everywhere. If we have not put down the answer to each peril as we have set it out, it is only because it would weary by repetition. Pray! Keeping close to God, we have the answer to all our needs.

Why is it that men who have most to say about the importance of prayer should sometimes pray so ill?

They lead exceedingly busy lives. It is not hard to persuade themselves that *doing* things is more important than praying about them. Three pastoral calls can be done in place of an hour of prayer. Several letters can be written. The prayer isn't so much cancelled in the mind as postponed—but it either comes to the same thing or is undertaken breathlessly. So the bloom goes off the spiritual life, and the busy little soul is laid open to all the perils we have enumerated above. In they troop! Prayer would have strangled them on the threshold. A guarded period of daily devotion would have ripped the disguises from all those dirty things and, in the white light of God, they would be seen for what they were.

Most ministers admit that they fail their people most in this. Their preaching and pastoral work may not be notable but they are more honestly undertaken than this secret praying. Superficially, the omission can pass unnoticed. Preachers are often thanked for their preaching, and the pastor's calls are pleasantly remarked upon, but only God knows the man who shuts the door and prays to the Father in secret.

God!—and the man himself—and, perhaps, a few discerning souls. Because (let there be no doubt about this) life is finer, and preaching is richer, and our influence over people is most assured, when we live near to God.

So pray! And then pray more! And on your most ineffective day, when you feel you have done so little, as you judge, for the Kingdom, comfort yourself that the day couldn't be ineffective because, whatever you have failed to do, *you have prayed*.

III

We come, finally, to certain perils which are more subtle than any we have named as yet. Indeed, it may be that only these could be called our 'occupational diseases' in the strictest sense of the term.

1. Preachers often *discharge a 'concern' by preaching a sermon on it*.

We all know what a 'concern' is. Our conscience is troubled. Whenever we are quiet before God, the matter comes up. It may be something in our private life, but it may be something in social, national, or international life. We feel that the grief of God is finding an echo in our own little hearts.

A well-instructed Christian layman knows what to do about it. If it is something in his private life, he must put it right. If it is something in social or national life, he shares it with his friends in the Christian fellowship, submitting himself to their correction or confirmation, and (if they come to share his concern) he can count on their aid in deciding, first, what must be done, and, then, how best to do it. Many of the great reformations of the world have begun in that simple way.

But it is just here that a peculiar peril of the preacher appears.

He gets 'concerns' too. Naturally! He is the minister of God. We should expect that the grief of God would find an early echo in his faithful heart.

But he is a *preacher* also. He is all the while appearing in public and exhorting people. A 'concern' is almost a gift to him. It is something to *preach* on and—here is the *quite awful* peril—having preached on it, his danger is to put it aside as though it had been 'dealt with'. The better he preaches on it, the more adequately he feels it has been 'dealt with'. God gave him the concern to *do* something about, and it has sprayed out in words.

Nor is this the worst aspect of it. There is some evidence for believing that, having preached on it, he is *less* likely to do anything about it. So far from the preaching assisting the toiling, it may militate against it.

Carlyle said: 'It is a sad but sure truth that every time you speak of a fine purpose, especially if with eloquence and to the admiration of by-standers, there is the less chance of your ever making a fact of it in your own poor life.'

How awful! This is an occupational disease indeed. Nobody else in the community is in the same dread danger as the preacher here, though politicians run the preachers close. Lloyd George said of Briand in the First World War: 'As soon as Briand descended from the rostrum he took no further interest in his speeches. For him speech was the same thing as action. At least his contribution to action ended with his perorations. It was for others to do the rest. If they neglected to do so, he was not to blame. . . .'[1]

What can a preacher do about this?

I can only share my own poor experience.

Being long aware of the danger, I have tried to make my own preaching part of my life. In the week preceding the Sunday, and during the days, therefore, when I have been preparing the sermons for delivery on that Sabbath, I have tried to make them autobiographical: to live in them: to incarnate in my own life the truths I was led to proclaim: to know the thing in experience before I uttered it in words. I have *tried* also to do something about it when the word was said.

God alone knows what success I have had in it. I am without confidence on the point myself. But this is one of the two most clear of our occupational diseases, and one which a man must watch both on his knees and on his face.

2. The other most clear of our occupational diseases is

[1] *War Memoirs of David Lloyd George*, pp. 2, 334f. (Ivor Nicholson and Watson).

the danger we are in from *people thinking us Christlike because they have got the help of Christ in our preaching*.

The error is pardonable but it is plain. The hungry souls come to worship on Sunday. Perhaps it has been a hard week with them. Low spirited but expectant, they bow their heads in God's house and then look up for food.

And God bends to their need: takes the word He has given to his minister, and nourishes their souls: lifts the depression right out of them, and sets them singing inside. How can they help but be glad? Is it surprising that they confuse the Source and the channel, and go to their minister with the words of thanks tumbling out as though *he* had given them the help?

Nor is it easy for the humblest man to set about 'correcting' every grateful soul. It seems pedantic and a little pedagogic also. Better by far that he bundle their sweet gratitude together and take it to God with apologies for his people's error, and God will delight in His servant's discernment and take the thanks of the people at second-hand.

The peril in all this arises in the possibility that a minister may suppose the thanks *belong* to him and accept them from the people as though by right. He may take it as a fitting tribute to his own industry and brilliance, and come to look for, and live on, the little words which are said.

We may leave it there. Glass-blowing, and coal-mining, and seafaring are all judged to be dangerous occupations. So is the Ministry of the Word. If we did not know that 'our sufficiency is from God' we should despair and abandon the task altogether. But we *do* know it, and go forward, therefore, unafraid.

INDEX OF NAMES